Endorsements

"Jim courageously witnesses to his own struggle while championing the Gospel that liberates life. That gives him authority to guide parents whose faith collides with the moral decisions of their children. Now a parent himself, Jim's story is a bridge for divided families. Jesus transforms—Jim helps us to believe Him for it!"

—Andrew Comiskey, Founding Director of Desert Stream Ministries, Kansas City, Missouri

"LGBT is not only a political issue; it is a personal and family heartache! Jim Domen's story is unique because he is authentic and candid with the harsh realities and details of the desperate relational neediness for acceptance as well as the corruption of indiscriminate sexual pleasure. His truthfulness helps dispel many myths, and this inspires the Church to improve Pastoral Care as well as believers to learn how to serve people like Jim with the love of Jesus. Family and friends, as well as mental health professionals, will appreciate the understanding of how Jim's parents assisted his Home Coming as well as Jim's growth in his masculinity through the love from his father. The revelation that Jim realized was, 'Jesus is my Savior, and my Lord!' Christian faith is an indisputable and transformative power (as always with people's struggles). Jim is happy with his life (I met him first in Taiwan while he was leading a Global 'Rainbow Crosser' Festival), my wife and I enjoyed his fellowship and leadership so much. On behalf of some like-minded movements around the world, 'Thank you, Jim, for leading us in the frontlines! We're so proud of you!' "

—**Melvin Wong, PhD,** 黃偉康博士
California Licensed Psychologist, San Francisco

"This endearing book is so intimately written that it almost feels like you're in it yourself, sometimes wiping tears, as you read about a family finding healing. It's a story about pain, the power of love, and the freedom that real honesty unleashes. As one of Jim's professors at Azusa Pacific University (Azusa, California), I can attest to the agony of his struggle and the truth of his resolve to choose life. His voice is crying out on behalf of everyone who longs to connect (not merely converse) with their father."

—**Sarah Sumner, PhD, MBA,**
President of Right On Mission, United States

"When it comes to faith and sexuality, one of the greatest needs in the Church is to have down-to-earth conversations where we 'speak the truth in love' (Ephesians 4:15). In his new book, my friend Jim Domen shares his personal story of brokenness, reconciliation, and redemption while honestly addressing those grappling with homosexuality. His vulnerability and transparency make this book a compelling testimony that will help break down barriers and restore compassion to what is often a polarizing topic. I believe *Not A Mistake* will impart hope for family members, friends, and individuals trying to navigate similar life experiences."

—**Senior Pastor Dr. Ché Ahn,**
Harvest Rock Church, Pasadena, California
President, Harvest International Ministry and
International Chancellor, Wagner University

"Jim Domen's book, *Not A Mistake*, finally puts to rest the trite Evangelical Christian response to same-sex attraction of 'love the sinner, but hate the sin.' Instead, we are presented with the only real response which aligns with the Gospel. Rather than focusing on attempting to change from 'gay to straight,' we are presented with Jesus Christ's invitation to ALL of us, irrespective of sexual inclination, which is to love the Lord with all our might, and to present our bodies as a living sacrifice. Jim Domen presents a candid portrayal of a Christian struggling with same-sex attraction. Domen's portrayal of his journey towards Jesus is one that all of us can relate to, especially for those of us who have struggled with sexual sin of any type. Regardless of your journey, *Not A Mistake* is essential to understanding the depth of Christ's love for you and his affirmation that you are 'Not a Mistake.' Amen!"

—Immigration Attorney Esther R. Valdés Clayton, Esq. Valdes & Associates, San Diego, California

"Jim Domen opens his heart and lets every reader experience his journey. This book is honest, gritty, and yet hopeful for every reader. Whether you are struggling with same-sex desires or someone you love is, this book will give you the tools to navigate your journey and God's promises to guide every conversation. As a pastor, I have dealt with this issue professionally. Thank you, Jim, for giving me this book, so I can care more effectively."

—Senior Pastor Rick Long, PhD, Grace Church, Arvada, Colorado

"There's no cheap triumphalism in *Not A Mistake*. This is hard-earned experience honestly shared that will cost Jim Domen and challenge those who oppose him. His concern to share boldly the grace he has found will inspire and encourage many who are finding new hope and freedom in their walk with Christ and His church. I recommend the reading of this book and am grateful for the effort Jim has made to be honest about his journey so far and what he still seeks to achieve."

**—Mike Davidson, PhD, Core Issues Trust,
United Kingdom**

"Because we live in a culture of confusion and misunderstanding, *Not A Mistake* provides a pathway, an actual model of hope. By inviting us into his story, Jim has provided a journey into his pain, loss, and confusion with such insight and revelation that hope begins to grab ahold of our hearts even before we experience his healing. This is an amazing resource that is not only timely but so deeply insightful that I would recommend it to every parent raising a child in today's world."

**—Senior Pastor Dr. Dan Carroll, Water of Life
Community Church, Fontana, California**

"In 2008, I met Jim at a news conference when the people of California voted and changed their Constitution to say that 'Only marriage between a man and a woman is valid or recognized in California' (Article 1 Section 7.5.) He's a fellow General and friend championing Truth in culture. His engagement in society dovetails with his heart and empathy for those who deal with LGBTQ issues and desire freedom. Pastor Jim's story is riveting and will help lead boys and men out of darkness. If you are a pastor, parent, or desire to understand leaving homosexuality, you'll be moved by his transparency as you journey alongside of him."

—Dr. Jim Garlow, CEO Well Versed, San Diego, CA

"Pastor Jim Domen has not only shared his incredible personal journey of brokenness to freedom and victory, but he has also provided a powerful template for parents, pastors, counselors, and those who feel helpless amid false sexual identities and behavior. His life exemplifies the true nature of the real battle against the 'LGBTQ+' false narrative that destroys lives physically, emotionally, and spiritually by leading us to a compassionate solution grounded in God's created order, the redemption available through Jesus Christ, and truth prevailing over the lie. I highly recommend *Not A Mistake* as a vital resource for all parents and anyone with this struggle or a desire to help themselves, their children, church members, and beyond as encouragement in understanding the 'why' as well as guidance with the 'how.' "

—Reverend Dave Welch, Founder and President, U.S. Pastor Council, Houston, Texas

"Pastor Jim Domen is a unique leader in the Christian Faith. His adherence to the Biblical mandates on human sexuality means that he has been persecuted and ostracized by the liberal Christians and secular humanist who have chosen to twist the bible to fit their cultural desires instead of allowing the Bible to shape culture. His book gives hope to those who struggle with sexual sin and have a desire to follow Biblical direction. He displays that God has an abundant plan for you that will exceed your innate human instincts when you follow His commands."

—Senior Pastor Dr. Robert Schuller, RobertSchullerMinistries.org, International

"The beauty of this book, it's for everyone. It's for those struggling with sexual desires and identity, as well as for friends and family who desire to understand those in the gay community and the brokenness that may have planted the seed.

"Throughout this book, Jim gives his personal account how from a young child, his hunger for acceptance and lack of love from his father turned him to find love from other men in the gay community. This book is a manual designed to provide the backstory of the journey for men and women who have chosen to exit the gay lifestyle. It was accomplished by a holistic approach to embrace a loving Christ-centered identity. This book destroys the myth that once gay always gay. Jim's story and many others have proven otherwise.

"Jim's book is a necessary read for individuals and families. It's for those who desire to gain understanding and hope to begin a loving journey to help restore and heal the broken relationships among the people we love."
—Bishop Ed Smith, Zoe Association International, Whittier, California

"Jim does not just tell his story, but in part three, he gives us much-needed practical steps and resources to help any individual or parent navigate through the struggle. The end of the book is filled with story after story of individuals that have found hope which is such an encouragement to any parent with a gay child. I highly recommend *Not A Mistake*. It would be a mistake for any individual or parent that has a child that is struggling with the issue of same-sex attraction to not read *Not A Mistake*."
—Senior Pastor Jim Franklin, Cornerstone Church, Fresno, California

"From the first time I met him, I have always admired the openness Jim has had to use his whole story for the glory of God and the good of others. Jim has always lived out the principle that the things we go through are never wasted by God as we use them to bring hope and encouragement to others. I am thrilled that Jim's story is now written down so that many others will be able to see God's faithfulness through Jim's life. In *Not A Mistake*, Jim weaves together personal experience and godly wisdom in order to speak tremendous hope and encouragement to both parents of men with same-sex attraction and to those wrestling with those attractions themselves. Jim has been able to write a book that is both accessible and yet void of the 'easy' answers and trite clichés that so easily can fill books of this nature—a rare feat that makes for an extremely valuable resource. I hope and pray that God is able to use this book in the same way that He has been able to use Jim himself in the lives of so many."

—Dr. Christopher Ward, DMin, Friends Church,
Yorba Linda, California

"I thank God for Jim Domen's bravery to lay out for us his homosexual journey and experiences in a way that is sensitive and caring for others to find hope, encouragement, and deliverance.

"This book is written in such a way that the reader should feel helped in understanding the struggles, pain, and rejection people battling with homosexuality or gender identity go through in life. Reading *Not A Mistake* helped me as a pastor gain insight into people with such struggles, but also the need for sensitivities parents and churches need to have when dealing with children or members who express such needs.

"The role of a counselor is important, but most important is the realization that God really loves people who struggle with homosexuality, and He is willing to help them gain their *true* identity rather than believing the stereotypes we all hear in society and among some of the people of God. The role of the family has an immense redemptive part in communicating love and acceptance to these people, even if it is very difficult to accept that lifestyle.

"This book will help honest people who are searching for answers to difficult questions. God will grant His Grace to all who *'seeking Him with all of their hearts.'* Prayer becomes an intricate part of the arsenal God has provided His children to battle day by day the difficult task of loving anyway!

"If you wish to gain insight into people who struggle with homosexuality, transgender confusion, and how to cope with daily issues of life, I recommend you read this book and use it as a helpful resource in ministry and in any other place God has called you to served Him or where you encounter people dealing with these issues.

"Thank you, Jim, for taking the time to write your story in such an understandable way that inspires hope to parents who love and want to help their children out of the hopelessness that this lifestyle cunningly invites so many of our Youngs. Your example tells us that you are secure in Jesus. May God continue to bless you by touching the many who need to discover and know that they ARE NOT A MISTAKE!"

—Senior Pastor Carlos Quintero, Iglesia Harvest Rock Hispana, Pasadena

"Jim Domen's book is so needed in a time like this to bring the other side of the story. Our culture portrays the "freedom," "equality," and "inclusiveness" of the Progressive movement, but they don't tell us what actually has happened to so many that just follow the crowd. Jim's testimony is one of hope and freedom not just for people struggling with same-sex attraction but also for all relatives and friends who love them and want to help them well. Thank you, Jim, for sharing your story with us with so much passion and biblical foundations!"

—Senior Pastor Netz Gomez, Houses of Light Church, Northridge, California Northridge House Of Prayer, Family Counselor and Good News For the Family Radio Show Host

NOT A MISTAKE

PARENTS' HOPE FOR THEIR GAY SON

JIM DOMEN

Foreword by Sean McDowell, PhD

VIDE

Vide Press
6200 Second Street
Washington D.C. 20011
www.VidePress.com

PB ISBN: 978-1-954618-38-1
eBook ISBN: 978-1-954618-39-8

Printed in the United States of America

To my parents John and Karen,
Who never gave up praying and knew how to celebrate
when I returned.

"'Quick! Bring the best robe and put it on him. Put a ring on his finger and sandals on his feet. Bring the fattened calf and kill it. Let's have a feast and celebrate. For this son of mine was dead and is alive again; he was lost and is found.'
So they began to celebrate."

—Luke 15:22-24 (NIV)

Table of Contents

FOREWORD   XIX

A NOTE TO PARENTS   XXI

PART 1 – MISTAKEN IDENTITY   1

Chapter 1: The Talk   3
Chapter 2: How Do I Tell My Parents I'm Gay?   13
Chapter 3: Not the Football Guy   23
Chapter 4: The Moment I Wanted to Die   35

PART 2 – MISTAKEN LOVE   47

Chapter 5: Coming Out   49
Chapter 6: Broke and Kicked to the Curb   61
Chapter 7: My Real Struggle with Identity   71
Chapter 8: Re-Adjusting to a Different World   79
Chapter 9: Learning to Be Completely Alone   91
Chapter 10: Healthy Male Sexuality   99
Chapter 11: Change Is Possible   107

PART 3 – UNMISTAKABLE HOPE   117

Chapter 12: A Divine Mistake   119
Chapter 13: Restoring the Years the Locusts Had Eaten   131
Chapter 14: The Battle Never Ends   139
Chapter 15: No Mistakes   153
Chapter 16: Dear Parent   165
Helpful Resources   173
Other People Who Are Not a Mistake   177

Foreword

By Sean McDowell

Have you ever felt like a failure as a parent? Have you ever experienced a loss of answers for how to respond in a parenting crisis? If the answer to either of these questions is "yes," then this book is for you.

While Jim writes through the lens of his personal experience growing up with same-sex attraction and how his parents responded to his "coming out," this book is for all parents who want to love their kids well. Whether you have kids who are LGBTQ or not, you certainly have friends who do. *Not a Mistake* will help all of us be prepared to respond well.

There are three big reasons I think you will love this book. First, *Not a Mistake* is based on Jim's personal experience. This is not merely an academic book (as important as those books are!) but a personal account from his own journey. And Jim doesn't hold back! While he offers theological and cultural insights, they are all filtered through his experience of growing up with same-sex attraction, living in gay relationships, and now parenting his three kids alongside his wife. This book is filled with fascinating stories and personal reflections.

Second, *Not A Mistake* is timely. The issue of LGBTQ relationships is front and center in the cultural conversation. All of us, and especially parents, are searching for biblically based resources on how to respond with love and kindness. Jim addresses all the big issues, such as the use of preferred pronouns, attending a gay wedding, and how to practically parent kids who identify as LGBTQ. He is committed to sharing what he believes is true, but always with a heart of compassion. I get daily emails from parents looking for resources on LGBTQ issues. Now I have a book I can recommend.

Third, *Not A Mistake* is countercultural. Whether in the media, educational system, Hollywood, or social media, we increasingly hear a singular voice about LGBTQ relationships and identities. If you stray from the common storyline, you may be threatened personally and professionally. As a result, many people choose to go along with the narrative. Yet, Jim refuses to be silent. You might disagree with some of his conclusions. But one thing is for sure—he will give you much to think about. His story deserves to be heard by anyone who values truth, inclusion, and open-mindedness. And this is especially true for parents who want to raise their kids to think critically.

Whether you have a child who identifies as LGBTQ or not, this book will give you hope, clarity, and conviction to love your kids with both grace and truth. Here's the bottom line—you are not a mistake. And neither are your kids.

Remember, the author of Hebrews reminds us that God will "equip you with everything good that you may do his will, working in us that which is pleasing in his sight, through Jesus Christ, to whom be glory forever and ever. Amen" (Hebrews 13:21, NASB).

—Sean McDowell, Ph.D., is a professor at Biola University, popular speaker, and the author of *Chasing Love: Sex, Love, and Relationships in a Confused Culture.*

A Note to Parents

It is not a mistake you picked up this book, and the fact that you are reading these words is an answer to my prayers.

For the past 15 years, I have had the privilege of sitting down with hundreds of parents whose sons have come out as gay. Most of these parents are Christians and know the basics of what the Bible says on topics such as homosexuality, and they are at a loss as to what to do. They feel distraught and hopeless. And from their vantage point, life has been a failure. The son they love is different in ways they did not imagine.

> I know the pain of being hurt, but I also know of handing it out to others.

Whenever I listen to moms and dads share these stories, my heart breaks inside and I can't help but think of my own journey. I remember that time when I pulled back from my parents for five years and pursued multiple gay relationships. This was a painful season, filled with moments of heartbreak. Moments like pulling up to my parents' home on the morning of December 25th, only to drop off presents without wishing them or my younger siblings a Merry Christmas.

I have been on both sides of the aisle. I know the pain of being hurt, but I also know the pain of handing it out to others. All of this gives me a unique perspective that I hope will prove helpful.

Because this topic is one that generates much controversy, even in the church, there are several points I feel should be clarified before we begin.

First, I write this as a man who has been changed. While some might celebrate being gay as part of God's design, I oppose that view. This is why I describe myself as a *Former* homosexual. Being gay used to be a part of my life, but it is no longer my story.

Second, the content I share might be more graphic than others who have written on similar topics such as this. Part of this speaks to my personality and straightshooter mentality. I want to tell it like it is. But in another sense, I share details with intention to give you an inside picture of what my journey was like.

> My purpose in writing is to provide hope and point you and your child to Jesus Christ as the only true source of identity.

Third, I want to elevate the conversation. Many in the gay community have been hurt by the language used by Christians. Author David Gushee writes, "It says something really terrible when the least safe place to deal with sexual orientation and identity issues is the Christian family and church."[1] I agree. Because of this, I want to be truthful in the words I articulate while also kind in my approach.

Fourth, my goal for this book is not to convert people from gay to straight. This book will only benefit those who want to change. If you picked up *Not a Mistake* with the hope I would outline some strategic formula that would change your son's desires, I am afraid you will be sadly disappointed. My purpose in writing is to provide hope and point you and your child to Jesus Christ as the only true source of identity.

Fifth, it is possible to learn new ways of thinking. I have encountered numerous individuals who were once attracted to the same sex but now find themselves only attracted to members of the opposite sex. In fact, I feature a number of these stories at the end of this book. Personally, I'm married to Amanda, and I choose to honor God, my wife, and our three children.

Sixth, I write this as a friend and a coach. While this book follows my story, in each chapter I pull back from the narrative and share the outlook I have today. I do this not to add confusion but to add perspective.

> **Your son is not a mistake.**

Seventh, your son is not a mistake. Right now, if you are in the beginning stages of your child's coming out, it is natural to blame yourself and be angry with the way things have gone. You find yourself looking in the mirror, wishing you had done things differently. My hope is this story makes you pause, step back, and see the larger picture of what God is doing. Yes, you might have made some mistakes, but your son and the relationship you have with him is not a mistake.

Nineteen years removed from my last gay partnership, if I were to journey back in a time capsule and offer a handwritten note to my parents on the outset of my coming out, this is what I would say.

Dear Mom and Dad,

I write to you because I want you to know what the future holds. There is hope. I know you are devastated right now. I just shared with you, that I, your first-born son, am gay. In this moment, your hopes, dreams, and aspirations for me have washed away.

I can see the heartache on your faces. I see the questions in your eyes. Deep down, you knew this was coming but you never wanted to believe it. The agony of not having grandchildren and the pain of not seeing me married to a woman are more than you can bear.

What about God's plan? What about my salvation? Where will I spend eternity? How will we all cope and respond? What are we to do? These are the questions I know you ask. I can also see you are embarrassed, asking yourself what our family members, friends, and church family will think.

But Mom and Dad, please do not give up on me. Pray and fast that God would disrupt my brokenness and lead me to healing, restoration, and transformation of mind, heart, and soul. The reason I made this decision is because I am so lonely and desperate to love. I want to love and want to be loved.

I know you will continue to worry about my salvation. Don't. Trust the words of God in Proverbs 22:6 (NIV), "Start children off on the way they should go, and even when they are old they will not turn from it." These words are true. Mom and Dad, God keeps His promises, and He is faithful beyond written explanation.

Dad, keep pressing in. Take time with me like you have never done before. I know it seems we have little in common, but find something I like to do and invest your time with me—even if it makes you uncomfortable in the process. I need my relationship with you.

Mom, I know you are a prayer warrior. Share with your trusted praying friends and intercede on my behalf. I need your prayers now more than ever. It seems impossible, but God will use this to bring me closer to Him and my testimony will help others. You will find joy in sharing your journey to help other parents going through this same journey.

Your son,
Jim

Part 1—Mistaken Identity

CHAPTER 1

The Talk

After months of evasion, my parents finally cornered me around our kitchen table to have *the talk*. "What is going on, Jim?" my mom asked with a look of concern spread across her face. "You're not acting like yourself. You live in our home, but you avoid us, rarely talk, and are gone all the time."

Coming out of a home that avoided any conversations slightly resembling the birds and the bees, I noted the concern on my parents' faces. By this point, my two younger siblings were out of the house. Jeff was in the middle of getting a law degree at Baylor Law in Texas, while Kim was taking advantage of a soccer scholarship at Cal State Long Beach.

"I met someone," I replied, recognizing my response generated more questions than it did answers. Hoping this would be the end of our conversation, I sat in silence, my anger rising by the moment. The year was 1999. I was 25 and at the start of a three-year relationship with my gay partner. Unbeknownst to my parents, several times a week I made the 90-minute commute from Anaheim Hills to where my partner lived in Palm Springs so we could spend time together.

"Met someone? Is this someone a woman or a man?" my mom questioned. The look on her face told me she already knew the answer.

"A man."

The man I referenced was my partner, "R." Although I had no intention of sharing these details with my parents at the time, R was HIV and Hepatitis C positive. At this point, however, I was so desperate to love and be loved that I did not care about his diagnosis. I wanted freedom to act upon the desires I had without feeling as though my actions would be questioned at every turn.

Short as my response was, those two words released a tidal wave of emotions into the small kitchen of our 2,000-square-foot Anaheim Hills bungalow. The life seemed to drain out of my mom as she sat in her chair, sobbing without control. And the warm Californian afternoon did little to thaw the icy silence that overcame my dad. For my parents, one a private Christian school librarian and the other a Los Angeles County Sheriff, their worst fear had become reality.

Their oldest child was gay.

In retrospect, this revelation should not have come as much of a shock. It certainly wasn't to those who knew me from a distance. Years later, many of my relatives confided in me that they knew I was gay, even when I was a teenager. It was obvious to them through my mannerisms, speech, likes, and dislikes.

Still living at home, I excused myself and slipped out of our kitchen and into my bedroom to call my sister. She was seven years younger than me but someone I could confide in and trust. After a few rings, she picked up the phone and answered from her dormitory room she shared with a few roommates. As soon as she did, she could sense my agitation.

"Jim, what's going on?" she asked. And from there, I explained the conversation I just had with our parents. As was the case with my mom, she also burst into tears. Her roommate, likely thinking I was a disgruntled ex-boyfriend, snatched up the phone and said, "Whoever this is, don't ever call this number again!" and hung up.

While coming out as gay is a more common occurrence in many households, my revelation came as a bombshell, and it threatened to destroy the very relationships with those who knew me best and loved me most.

GROWING UP IN AN ANTI-GAY HOUSEHOLD

To understand my parents' response, there is some historical context that needs to be outlined. My mom and dad were both Christians. Every time the doors of our 1,200-seat church sanctuary were open, we were there. Sunday School, Vacation Bible School, Youth Group, you name it. That was our life, and my parents did everything they could to help their kids grow up to love and serve Jesus.

Not only that, but my mom and dad were active in sharing their faith with others and taking a stand against cultural movements that stood against their understanding of Biblical principles. For example, in the 1980s, two such movements were abortion and homosexuality.

Each were viewed with a similar degree of repulsion. Abortion destroyed the life God created, whereas homosexuality desecrated the model God established for how life should be lived.

To my mom's horror, she discovered local schools could not even give a 17-year-old girl an aspirin, but they could offer her options for having an abortion. When I was in high school, I remember taking the "Walk for Life for the Unborn" with my mom in Santa Ana, California, going from one abortion clinic to the next. I even took my youth pastor to stand outside of an abortion clinic in Pacoima, California. This cause was very important to me, and I saw it as an opportunity to save lives.

As for the so-called "homosexual movement," my parents were joined at the hip in their strong opposition. Because my dad was a Los Angeles County Sheriff's Deputy, he was called on to work numerous pride parades. Each time this happened, he was sickened by what he witnessed—believing it was a blatant display of arrogance against God.

There was no ambiguity in my mind as to what my parents believed on these two issues. And due to their strong opposition, it would seem improbable that any of their kids would wind up supporting either of these two positions. But in the words of my mom, Satan knew her Achilles' heel. And within the span of a couple years, she would not only discover her oldest son was a homosexual, but she would also find out her only daughter had chosen to have an abortion. Both revelations came nearly 20 years after she led both of us to faith in Christ.

My sister was six when she made this commitment, and I was the tender-hearted age of four. My early years of childhood development saw me become a posterchild for the Christian faith. On more than one occasion, I remember one of my teachers making a remark that I would make a great missionary one day.

I say all this to point out that, even though my parents should have seen my revelation coming, there was good reason for them to be surprised. They could not deny the turn my life had taken, but deep down they still thought of me as their sensitive young son who wanted nothing more than to love and serve Jesus.

It's safe to say that both were in a state of shock. "We felt so sad," my mother recalled. "You had been struggling alone with same-sex attraction for years, and you had no one to come alongside and support you."

Neither of them knew how to respond. In the words of my mom, "I felt all of the life drain out of me. I was empty, helpless, numb, confused, and could not stop crying." My dad, on the other hand, had a different reaction. He was embarrassed and did not want my mom to share my coming out with anyone. And as one could imagine, this only made life harder on my mom who desperately needed the prayer and emotional support. She honored my dad's wishes however, and did not tell anyone else about my story until I had officially *crossed over*.

By this point, she was still an emotional mess. The strong bond she once held with her oldest son was broken.

BRIDGING THE COMMUNICATION GAP

It's hard to know what to say when you feel devastated. Now that I am a parent, I understand a taste of what my parents must have gone through on that day. I picture one of my children having a conversation like this with me, and I can only imagine all of the pain and emotions that might run through my mind.

"What did I do wrong?"

"I am a failure as a parent."

"God will never forgive me."

Several years ago, Pew Research conducted a study of 1,197 LGBT (Lesbian, Gay, Bisexual, and Transgender) adults and discovered that 39% of them stated that when they shared their coming out with friends or family, they experienced rejection by someone close to them.[2] This says there is still a sizeable group of parents who find this news earthshattering and do not know how to cope with this change. You might be one of them.

All of this begs the question—how do you bridge the gap of communication? What do you say to a child when you feel your relational bond with them is broken?

From my observation, most of the communication gaps adult children have with their parents stem back to the fact that they were never properly instructed how to communicate.

Most parents do not *grease the wheels* before they have conversations about topics around sexuality and resort to taking one of three harmful approaches:

A. They talk so freely about the subject that human sexuality is trivialized.
B. They avoid the subject altogether and hope for the best.
C. They talk about sex with their kids but do so in an awkward manner.

My childhood was a cross between B and C. There were times we talked about sex and relationships, but these conversations were always done at discreet moments with little follow up. I was expected to figure life out as I went along.

As a father of three kids, this is a conversation my wife and I have often as we raise our children. From a young age, we've wanted our kids to feel comfortable talking to us about any questions they have. For example, we have taken the lead from our friend Dr. Jim Burns (author of *God Made Your Body*) and initiated conversations with our kids about their body parts as early as their first birthday.

This conversation has never been awkward for our kids because it has not been awkward for us. Boys have a penis, and girls have a vagina. It is not uncomfortable or weird and is sometimes even comical!

Soon after my son turned three, we happened to have a few guests over to the house for supper. That's when he took note of our male dog's anatomy and exclaimed, "Dad! There's Tucker's penis!" This gave all of us a good laugh.

My point is not to be crude but to emphasize the importance of communication. Every open interaction you have with your children when they are young lays a framework for them to be open with you when they grow up. I want my kids to come and talk to me when they have questions, but I also know the only way this will happen is if they feel safe to have these conversations.

I have discovered that lack of communication breeds suspicion and creates confusion. Connection is key for every parent and child relationship. Author John Maxwell likes to say, "Everyone communicates, few connect."[3] He is exactly right. It's not about having mere conversations with our kids about sports and fun activities. It's about having meaningful dialogue where we seek to learn and gain perspective. We live life with them, so they hear what we are saying and know that we are listening.

It is important to note that if you have not done the hard work of establishing communication with your children, there is no time like the present to start. Do not skip this step. If you launch into a conversation on the nature of their sexual identity without first seeking to connect, it will not be long before you find yourself in an argument.

Instead, if your relationship with your child has been broken, take time to listen to his perspective. Hear where he is at. Instead of offering your opinion, understand this moment in your life is one of the greatest opportunities you will have to be Jesus with skin to those you love.

Rather than trying to find some sort of short-term resolution in the moment, begin the process of repairing communication. This might include attending a concert with him, going on a nature hike, or sitting down to watch his favorite TV show. At this point, it's not about the activity. It is all about the relationship.

THREE STEPS TO HAVING *THE TALK*

As your communication gap is bridged, you can seek more clarity. Part of the way you gain clarity is by clearly articulating what you believe to be true. If you do not do this, you will wind up relying on your feelings to dictate your response. And as most people know, feelings can be fickle.

Here is what I suggest. If your child approaches you and says they believe he is gay, my friend Joe Dallas offers three helpful clarifying positions.[4]

First, clarify your son or daughter's position. It is possible his coming out might be a point of confusion. I have worked with several individuals who thought that one homo-erotic experience meant they were gay. But this was not the truth. They had an experience that was not natural for them but have since continued to have heterosexual feelings and emotions.

Such was the case for my friend "S." In his early developmental years, S's father died and his mom chose to remarry someone who turned out to be a sexual predator. More than once, S suffered sexual abuse at the hands of his new dad. The very person who was supposed to be his protector turned out to be his molester. Because of all he experienced, S thought he must be gay.

When we met, I listened to S's story, and my heart broke for him. But after I heard what he had to say, I looked him in the eyes and said, "S, what occurred to you was evil. Dads should protect their families, and your dad was not able to protect you. What happened to you was not your fault. It should have never happened. You are not gay. Someone abused you sexually. You are a heterosexual man." I will never forget the look of relief that spread across S's face. What he needed was someone to speak truth and hope into his life. This might be where your child is.

But if your child says he has experienced same-sex attraction for an extended period, it is important to understand his perspective. Does he believe acting on his desires is wrong? Is he asking you to join him in celebrating his new identity and the lifestyle that is often associated with this identity? What is his view of having a healthy sexuality?

Second, clarify your own position. It is important to know where you stand on this matter and not allow your viewpoint to be swayed by emotion. Because we love our kids, it can be easy to want to pair our beliefs with theirs and go with the popular mantra, "Blood is stronger than theology."

If you do not know what you believe, this is where it is time to do your homework. Go to God's Word, seek out helpful resources, and talk with a Bible-based pastor and counselor. Please make sure to vet the pastor or counselor. You need to know their views on sexuality beforehand. As you do this, you will find there are likely some misconceptions you held that need to be challenged.

Third, clarify your fears. What are you afraid of? Are you fearful your child's soul is lost? Do you worry about him or her becoming HIV positive? It is important that you identify your fears, however irrational they might seem. Doing so allows you to deal with all of the stress and anxiety you face.

At this point, you are still his parent, but you are also his friend. Love your child. Feel his pain and agony. There is a good chance he is just as fearful as you are. Let him know you are there for him, regardless of what decisions are made, and you will never abandon him.

Give your child the gift of presence. Choose to love him even when doing so feels difficult. Seek to know the backstory that led him to announce he is gay. As you do, your sympathy and understanding will increase, and you will then be able to do as Ephesians 4:15 instructs and speak the truth in love.

In our next few chapters together, I will take you behind the scenes of my own personal journey that prompted my coming out. And it is my prayer that through reading my story, you can find hope for your child's journey. His life is not a mistake, and there is hope.

CHAPTER 2

How Do I Tell
My Parents I'm Gay?

Elementary school was when I first realized I was *different*. While still in the third grade, I remember joining some of my neighborhood friends in their backyard playhouse, only to discover a treasure trove of *Playboy* magazines. I remember looking at this stack of pictures of nude women and feeling unfazed. There was little to no attraction.

By way of contrast, several months later, I rode my bike to a neighborhood hangout called Tuffree Park. At the time, much of the area was undeveloped, but there was a huge cluster of trees at one part of the park that was surrounded by green rolling hills. This area allowed kids to be alone and have some privacy. There among the branches I found a few torn up pieces of a *Playgirl* type of magazine.

This time my reaction was different.

Looking at the various images of naked men, I found myself aroused in a way I had never experienced before. For the first time in my life, the thought crossed my mind, *Maybe I am gay*. I stress the word *thought* because there was no way I was ever going to express this out loud.

Keep in mind this was the 1980s, and the general public was still trying to figure out how to treat people who iden-tified as homosexual (the dreaded ten-letter word). Tack on to that all of the conversations surrounding AIDS, and there was general panic that simply being *around* someone who identified as gay could cause you to catch an unwanted disease. Stating you were gay in the 80s did not carry with it the weight of pride that it carries in many communities today.

I remember traveling with my family to my grandmother's home in Buena Park, California, to visit my Uncle Mark shortly before his death of AIDS in 1986. Overshadowing this funeral was a cloud of embarrassment and shame. No one wanted to talk about it. It was all just awful.

As an eleven-year-old kid, I remember visiting Uncle Mark before his death and making sure I kept my distance. I didn't want to use the same toilet seat, hold anything he had touched, or sit too close to him at supper. To my irrational young mind, knowing I had these attractions to men made me think to myself, *Hey, I'd better be careful because this must mean I am more susceptible to catching AIDS.* To this day, Uncle Mark's death is seldom talked about in my extended family.

Fear permeated my thoughts, and I felt as though I had no safe place to express, share, or vent my concerns. How could I explain to others what I was processing in my mind? Who would listen? Who would care?

I must be some sort of mistake.

A SEVENTH GRADER'S CRY FOR HELP

Just the thought of being gay repulsed me to my core. Still, I could not argue with the feelings I experienced.

As a young boy, I remember those times in seventh grade when I did my best to *pray the gay away*, "God, I don't like the way I feel! I hate that I have these desires that seems like only I can understand." But despite my best prayers and times spent reading the Bible, nothing changed. My sexual urges remained the same. I felt helpless and did not know where to turn.

14

Being raised in a Christian family, I knew things like looking at pornography were not healthy and were also seen as sinful. But this knowledge did little to stymie the fascination I felt, and I could not escape the question—why do I want *this* and not *that*?

As I grew older and entered seventh grade, I began to crack and open up about my struggle with others. The first person I told was a youth worker named Jenny.

During the winter, my parents sent me to Forest Home for our church's junior high camp. Forest Home was a church retreat center located in the San Bernardino Mountains just 40 miles down the mountain from Big Bear Lake. It was a historical mecca of sorts for the Christian community, as influential Christian figures such as Henrietta Mears and Billy Graham had spiritual encounters at this same camp. To me, the San Bernardino Mountains felt like home. They were a place where I could collect my thoughts and spend time alone with God.

After wrapping up one of our afternoon activities, I knew I needed to talk with somebody. Avoiding the tall, dark-haired, and well-built youth pastor and the young, handsome, and blonde male youth worker, I turned my attention to a young and care-free girl named Jenny.

"Hey, I need to talk with you," I blurted out.

Jenny paused what she was doing and looked up, "Sure Jim, what is on your mind?"

Collecting my thoughts, I asked if we could take a walk. At an elevation of 3,500 feet, Forest Home Camp is like a sanctuary at night, and the starry-lit sky made for an impressive backdrop. As we strolled into the darkness, outside of earshot of my fellow campers, I shared my secret with Jenny.

"Look, Jenny, I've been praying a lot, and I think I am homosexual."

Jenny said nothing at first and just listened. She was in an awkward spot. I could tell she cared which meant a lot, but neither of us knew what to do. After all, she was a college-aged intern with our junior high department and not used to hearing this kind of "confession."

After a few minutes, Jenny called over the youth pastor and asked me to share with him what I had just told her. "Jim, this sounds like a big conversation," he said. "How about we talk about this back at church when we get off the mountain?" I agreed.

But aside from one brief conversation I had with him in his office, we never spoke on this subject ever again. And while this exchange was helpful and it felt good to get the secret off my chest, the internal struggle in my mind continued to grow.

SHARING WITH MY FRIEND

How I wish I could go back in time and open up with someone else who could have provided help. I needed counseling to process my emotions. The last thing I needed to do was sweep my feelings underneath the rug. But that was exactly what I would do for the next three years until my sophomore year of high school.

I maintained my image as the perfect child who never broke any rules. If anything, I bordered on being a bit of a snitch. Instead of hanging out with the kids who were athletic and cool, I found my own tribe of academics who were part geek and part nerd. Our snobbish philosophy was, "Hey, we're not as cool as you, but you will be cutting our lawns one day!"

Up until this point, I had not had one conversation with my parents about this topic. Everything was kept quiet, and any time subjects like homosexuality and sex were brought up in our home, the conversation was quickly squelched and shifted to something else. But when I turned 16, these internal struggles spilled out into a conversation with my friend "K."

"I don't know what to do," I shared one afternoon. "I keep having these urges to lust and masturbate over men." Being the good friend that he was, K pointed me to our youth pastor, D Clark, whom I count as a friend to this day. I shared with him the feelings I had, and he gave me a piece of advice I wished I'd received years sooner: "Jim, you need to tell your parents."

TELLING MY PARENTS THE FIRST TIME

The reason my coming-out story in chapter one should not have been a surprise to my parents was because there was a similar talk we had almost a decade previously. And this conversation turned out much differently than I expected.

"Mom, Dad, I need to tell you something." The year was 1990, and I was in the 10th grade. I intentionally picked a time of day when both my younger siblings were not around so just the three of us could talk in private. My dad assumed I wanted advice on a new female relationship.

Not knowing where to begin, I decided to come out and say it. "I think I am a homosexual. I keep reading God's word and praying, but nothing changes."

"How long have you been dealing with this?" my dad wondered.

"Since seventh grade."

Upon sharing this, something odd and overwhelming happened. My dad was stunned and cried for the first time I had ever witnessed in my life. And not just a tear or two. He absolutely wept. This was a side of him that was unknown to me, and I was not sure how to respond.

We all sat there in awkward silence as his cries carried through our home. Dad would later tell me the reason he got so emotional was because he felt horrible that I had carried this weight so long by myself. Adding to the weight he felt was a sense of helplessness, not knowing anything to say or do that could help. As my dad would later tell me, he cried himself to sleep every night for the next several weeks—not out of pity for himself, but for me.

As a law enforcement officer, he dealt with many in the gay community. Having the heart for people that he had, Dad made it a point to pause and listen to their stories whenever he could, and the story was often a familiar one. A kid grew up in an abusive home with little parental guidance which resulted in him being gay.

But when his own son came forward with this admission, he did not know what to do, and his thoughts immediately shifted to what he had done wrong.

In retrospect, I have a ton of sympathy for my parents. Both of them came from households that did not talk about anything related to sex. As a result, when it came time to raise their own kids, my parents did the best they knew how with the training they received. And even though the relationship with my parents was not what I would have liked, and despite the fact that this would be one of the few conversations we would ever have on this topic until my coming out nine years later, that interaction forever changed the way I looked at my dad.

To this day, I continue to be touched by my father's response and the heart he showed for me as his oldest child.

TURNING TO COUNSELING

Coming out of that initial conversation with my parents, I told them I wanted to visit a counselor to process my thoughts. They agreed, and we scheduled an appointment with a therapist recommended by my youth pastor. For the next two years, "T" and I met together and explored what it meant to pursue what I call healthy male sexuality.

I was excited to meet T and connect with someone who could help me process and hopefully change my homosexual desires. Through our time together, I began to see the root causes of my same-sex attraction and connected some of the dots in my own life. I recognized the great disconnect I had with my dad and areas of improvement that needed to change with my mom. This process helped my mind rest and not be in anguish because I had someone who could help me walk through my internal battles and struggles.

During those two years until I turned 18, my parents scarcely mentioned the subject again. Following my weekly visits with T, they seldom inquired how things were going or how I was doing. It was kind of that whole "don't ask, don't tell" culture.

I remember wanting to talk about my experiences with Dad, but the furthest we ever got was him asking, "How was your time with T?" This was followed by my one-word response, "Good." He was always quick to move on to the next topic as though doing so would make the whole situation go away.

T was seldom mentioned at home, and none of my immediate family members, extended family, or friends knew who he was. T was a secret, and I was instructed never to tell anyone that we met.

This point was emphasized on the one occasion I slipped up. I remember meeting one of eight chiefs within the Los Angeles Sheriff's Department—just two ranks away from sheriff. And after my dad introduced me to his boss' boss' boss' boss—the chief asked me the offhanded question, "How are you doing, and what are you learning in high school?" I beamed and proudly shared I was going to counseling and meeting with a therapist. My dad was horrified, and I received a stern talking-to after the meeting. The message was clear. We don't *ever* share topics like counseling or therapy with other people.

> They tolerate a right to change but not a right to choose.

Sadly, this cultural viewpoint continues to manifest itself in California politics today with many politicians attempting to make it illegal for teens to go to a counselor and receive the sort of help I experienced. In their minds, kids like me should have the choice to be gay, bisexual, or transsexual, but we should not have the option to choose heterosexuality. Kids can seek to alter their biological sex from male to female, but they cannot decide to pursue therapy for same-sex attraction. In an odd way, they tolerate a right to change but not a right to choose.

I will devote more time to this topic later, but it bears repeating that my time in counseling was my choice, very helpful, and quite different from how such therapies are represented by many media outlets across the nation.

WHAT I WISH

Looking back on my childhood, I wish honest conversations on this topic could have been an option. The cloak of secrecy made me live in two different worlds—the worlds of reality and fantasy.

My fantasy world said, "Jim, what would it be like to have a boyfriend? Imagine having a close friend with whom you could share your thoughts and dreams."

Reality said, "Jim, you can't talk about any of this stuff with other people. They will laugh at you, call you names, or disassociate from you." Indeed, that was a fair point.

Today, making gay jokes has become culturally taboo—thank goodness. But in those days, gays were cannon fodder for would-be comics who wanted to get a good laugh. Phrases like, "You're so gay!" or "He's such a faggot!" were common. And sadly enough, these phrases were quite common in Christian circles. More than once, I heard my friends make disparaging remarks about gay people. And each time I heard one of these comments, I couldn't help but think to myself, *They're talking about me!*

All I could think when I heard these statements was, *Jim, keep your mouth shut. Don't say a word, and hopefully no one will ever know.*

It is hard to express how deep this pain can be. To have those who are close to you make statements that disparage who you believe you are cannot help but feel like the ultimate condemnation. Today, as I speak with parents of gay children, I often hear them say something like this, "Jim, before understanding my child, I just never realized how much my words hurt." As authors Greg and Lynn McDonald write, "When you have a gay child, you suddenly become aware of how often people say things at the expense of others."[5]

Going through those painful years as a child have made me much more sensitive to the hurts of others. I have come to realize that many people in this world suffer in silence. It is for this reason I have committed my life to speak on behalf of those who are vulnerable and lack the voice they need. I know what a difference even one voice could have made in my life during such a pivotal period of time. I was alone, I was scared, and I was fearful.

> Be like my dad and cry, not for yourself but for your child.

Parents, if your child has suffered in silence for years, recognize what a huge act of courage it took for him to open up with you. Be like my dad and cry, not for yourself but for your child. Do not bemoan the embarrassment of what this revelation might be for you but see it as an opportunity to be like Jesus.

There is a good chance your child feels like he is an oddity—a mistake. It is your job to show him he is not.

CHAPTER 3

Not the Football Guy

I was never known as the rough and tumble guy in our neighborhood. Even from a young age, I would describe myself as a *sensitive soul*, kind of like Pumba—the warthog from the *Lion King*.

I wasn't a big fan of run and gun crime shows and instead preferred softer TV programs like *Little House on the Prairie*. One of my favorite shows was *CHiPS*. And as I watched, I felt myself drawn to a California Highway Patrol officer named John. In my mind, he exemplified what it meant to be masculine. Ironically, even though my own father had a law enforcement background, I did not connect with him as my example of masculinity.

> The whole idea of what it meant to become a man was strange to me.

The whole idea of what it meant to become a man was strange to me. On one hand, I knew what everyone around me said about boys being attracted to girls, but despite this fact, I could not escape my internal desire to connect with men. More than anything, I desperately wanted a best friend. In the fourth grade, I begged God to send another boy my age into my life so we could hang out and do the things typical boys my age liked to do.

But this never happened. Instead, I was engulfed in femininity. And while I received a good deal of empathy, none of my masculine qualities were brought to the surface. A couple months ago, I was watching an old video of me in fourth grade, holding one of my younger cousins in my arms. Everything about my stance was so "gay." My hips were tilted, and my wave was effeminate. As I watched, I couldn't help but shake my head. Why didn't anyone help me? Why didn't one person show me what manhood looked like or how real men behaved?

> Why didn't anyone help me?

I spent most of my childhood hanging out with girls instead of boys, even into high school. After football games on Friday nights, I always spent time with older girls who were juniors and seniors in high school. In my mind, they were more comfortable and safer to hang around. Sure, I remember playing with boys my age and having dirt clod wars, but this never developed into friendships that met my inner needs.

That said, like most boys who play rough, I did enjoy wrestling. I recall wrestling with my friend "B" during our elementary school years one day and getting slightly aroused in the process. It was very confusing, but I knew there was something about that interaction that I liked. B was the big, rough, and tough kid—the bully on the street, while I was the softer, more effeminate kid.

Sports and I did not mesh well. When I was in first grade, I tried T-ball and turned out to be a decent hitter. However, I had one major flaw to my game—I was scared of the ball! I was constantly afraid of getting hurt. Soccer wasn't much better, and my respect for goalkeepers increased. Who in their right mind would volunteer to have people kick balls at them for fun?!

It was not until later that I would understand why I reacted the way I did.

FRESHMAN YEAR OF FOOTBALL

Despite my aversion to sports, it did not stop me from trying. My dad said I needed to pick one sport and stick with it. Since sports were almost viewed as a rite of passage in our household and I was desperate to please my dad, I did what any son in my situation would do—I joined football.

In 1988, I entered my freshman year of high school. And like the young jock who signed up for the army but prayed to God he would never experience combat, I signed up for the football team, just hoping I could avoid catching a pass or receiving a hit. This prompted me to try out for the free safety position.

I was terrible from the start. In fact, my problems started in the dressing room before we ever

> **I was desperate to please my dad.**

stepped foot on the gridiron. First, it was filled with a bunch of boys my age undressing, and that was awkward enough. Even though I wasn't that attracted to the guys on my team, the whole environment felt weird. Making matters worse, I had no idea how to put on the equipment. The shoulder pads were confusing, and I couldn't help but think a sport that required this amount of protection was probably not a sport that would make me want to "hit 'em harder."

For our team picture at the start of the school year, I stood next to our coach, because he told the team that players who stood next to him *would* make it as football players. But he had no idea who Jim Domen was, and his prophetic word turned out to be inaccurate. Instead of being a standout free safety, I spent most of that season on the bench.

That first week was the infamous *Hell Week*. I nearly died. We had to run and hit these massive sleds and push them back together as a unit. I still remember doing my best to approach them as timidly as possible. Still, I stuck with it, and despite my aversion to being hit, I enjoyed the team atmosphere. I liked being around a group of guys who were on my side, even if there were times they might try to take my life.

My friend "B" was an animal. He was massive, and every practice I pictured my frail frame flattened underneath his weight. My only saving grace was that he was a Christian and believed in the seventh commandment—thou shalt not murder. Then there was "M"—a medium-build, stocky kid whose fierce looks were almost as intimidating as his thunderous hits. My friend "D" was another great guy and even became a Christian later in life. But at that time, his look alone could knock you over.

> My fear of being hit by humans or balls made me the type of guy wide receivers and running backs loved to face.

I, on the other hand, was 132 pounds soaking wet. This did not make me the smallest guy on our team, but I was one of the weakest. My frame and mannerisms were no match for the tough players on our team, and my fear of being hit by humans or balls made me the type of guy wide receivers and running backs loved to face. When they saw me, their eyes lit up. Instead of being an impediment to their destination, I was more like a gatekeeper. "Thank you for playing today, and welcome to the endzone!" could have been my catchphrase.

It was not until the fourth or fifth game that I got on the field for some actual playing time. We were up by 40 points with only minutes remaining on the clock. Not even I could have messed that one up.

To my dad's credit, he never said a word to discourage me. Every game, he would sit in the stands while I sat on the bench. And on those rare occasions I did make it into the game, I remember him screaming something like, "Just hit 'em!"

I seldom took his advice.

MY RELATIONSHIP WITH MOM

Part of my problems came back to the strong relationship I had with my mom and the weak relationship I experienced with my dad.

Recently, my mom and I were watching my wife take care of our eighteen-month-old son when Mom commented, "You know, Jim, when you were that age, you only wanted me and were completely attached to me, almost in an unhealthy way." Her statement unearthed another key to my understanding of same-sex attraction.

Mom and I had a tight relationship. When I was seven and my mom was pregnant with my sister and suffering morning sickness, I would watch out for her when my dad was at work. In an odd way, I was her caregiver. It was natural for me. I loved to care for others. I was sensitive and emotionally connected.

> This deep connection I felt with my mom caused me to mimic her feminine qualities while my opportunity to learn masculine traits fell by the wayside.

This deep connection I felt with my mom caused me to mimic her feminine qualities while my opportunity to learn masculine traits fell by the wayside. Not only did Mom and I connect on an emotional level, but we also related on a spiritual level. She was the one who led me to the Lord, and on those days when Dad was gone, she became more than my mom. She was my friend.

Puberty hit around sixth grade, and I was a mess. The first time I saw hair grow on my testicles, I was afraid I had a disease. But rather than have a conversation with my dad, I showed my "problem" to my mom. At that point, the right move for my mom would have been to invite my dad into the conversation, but she didn't. This only heightened my dependency on her.

> While neither my mom nor I thought about it at the time, all of these moments spent together created an unhealthy sense of dependency that heightened my connection with her and diminished what little connection I had with Dad.

Around that same time, I remember feeling discouraged on many days and visiting the private Christian school library where my mom worked. I told her about some of the problems I was facing, and she said I could always come and spend time with her.

As my body grew and developed, so did my fears. I was apprehensive about shaving, and the idea of dating was the furthest thing from my mind. I felt so insecure around other boys my age that I could not talk about girls.

While neither my mom nor I thought about it at the time, all of these moments spent together created an unhealthy sense of dependency that heightened my connection with her and diminished what little connection I had with Dad.

MY RELATIONSHIP WITH DAD

I do not want to create the impression that my dad never tried to connect with me. It's quite the opposite in many respects.

Dad was a good man who was trying to do the best he knew how. There were times we had fun together. I still remember going with my dad in his 1970 Nova back when you could stand up on the bench seat (remember those days?). We would drive to get ice cream together with my arm wrapped around his shoulders. My dad loved chewing tobacco, so we would often end up stopping by this place called Vendome to replenish his supply. To this day, whenever I walk into a humidor or get a whiff of tobacco, it takes me back to my early childhood. At four years of age, I was still too little to open the sliding door to the store and would have to wait for Dad to give me a hand. Those were some fond memories!

My dad never abused or hurt me in any way. He was a good man, a good cop, and someone who was fair. That said, while we did have several fond moments together, it is important to note that doing fun things is not an adequate replacement for building a healthy relationship. I think my dad thought he had more influence in my life than he actually had. He was always quick to share his opinion, and I've often said that if I had a nickel for every time my dad gave me advice, I would be a wealthy man.

> Doing fun things is not an adequate replacement for building a healthy relationship.

And much as I respected my dad, I still possessed an unhealthy fear. In psychology, there is a term called defensive detachment disorder. This is magnified when a circumstance or situation arises when a father speaks harshly to his son. It might be an embarrassing or shaming moment, and the result is the son shuts off his relationship with his dad. A child is not cognizant of what's happening, but to protect himself, he turns off his father-son relationship. This means that even when the father exhibits love or healthy affection, it is not received.

From a personal standpoint, characteristics such as my dad's aggression, firmness, and strength tended to scare me because I had a sensitive heart. Those times he pointed his finger at me or poked me in the chest were moments I wanted to wither and crawl under a table. (It probably did not help that Dad always carried his gun with him everywhere he went!)

> While this hardened approach might have connected well with some boys, it only drove me further into the arms of my mother for safety.

I remember one time we were driving down our street, and some kid in another car did something foolish. It caused my dad to throw open his door and almost physically remove the teen from his vehicle. I was terrified, but that was my dad. One of his positions with the LA County Sherriff's department was to serve as a drill sergeant at the sheriff's academy. He was used to giving orders and having people take his advice to heart.

Those who knew my dad from a professional work relationship could not believe he was someone who would have kids of his own! And while this hardened approach might have connected well with some boys, it only drove me further into the arms of my mother for safety.

WHEN YOUR CHILD HAS DIFFERENT DESIRES

One of the greatest challenges of parenting well is going to where our kids are emotionally and meeting them at *their* points of need.

For my dad, he easily connected with my younger brother because they shared a set of common interests. However, I was someone who found joy in life out of a whole different set of experiences, and my dad did not know how to respond.

For example, one afternoon I was in the backyard with my parents, and I mentioned to Dad that I wanted to learn French.

"French?" he asked, "Why wouldn't you take Spanish?"

I responded that I wanted to visit France one day and see the world. And indeed, this conversation served as a foreshadowing of the many adventures I would have. As of this writing, I have visited over 40 different countries and find it fascinating each time I travel to a new area.

But to my dad who saw no good reason to leave California, this made little sense. Why learn a new language, tour the world, and experience new adventures when you already have a great life and live in a beautiful area? We just thought about life from very different perspectives.

Today, I have the privilege of speaking to hundreds of parents, many of whom have children who are same-sex attracted. When this revelation is discovered, many feel like it is a death sentence, and it's as though their greatest fears have become reality. My response is to put a different perspective on their greatest fear. Having a child come out as gay *is* a sort of death sentence, but not in the way you might think. As my friend Joe Dallas notes, having a gay child brings about a death of expectations.[6]

> Having a gay child brings about a death of expectations.

That picture you had for your perfect family where all your kids would grow up, get married, bring home grandbabies, and live happily ever after is shattered, and you do not know how to put the pieces back together.

When this happens, many parents resort to doubling down on their best efforts and intentions. They continue to try to connect with their kids in the one way they have always tried because that is all they know. The rough dad continues to push his effeminate son, thinking things will change if he can just get him in the right environment.

But this is where our faith in God comes into play and gives us some direction. The heart of the Gospel message is that we serve a God who has come down to meet men and women where they are. A quick scan of Scripture shows you that God meets people in their broken state and works with them in the midst of their mess.

> Our God goes to where people are, and every parent should follow His example.

He met Jacob the conniver, Moses the murderer, David the adulterer, Rahab the prostitute, and Paul the persecutor (among others) exactly at their greatest point of shame. And as Romans 5:8 notes, "While we were still sinners, Christ died for us."

Our God goes to where people are, and every parent should follow His example.

If you have a child with desires and passions that do not align with yours, you have a wondrous opportunity to embrace the incarnate Christ who laid aside all of the pleasures and joys of heaven to be born in a stable among messed-up men and women who would seek His death.

If you are a parent, it does not mean you will have to leave behind a kingdom of gold to be born in a stable, but it might mean giving up a couple evenings a week to spend one-on-one time with your kids. Fathers, it might mean taking your son out for a night on the town to see a theatrical performance. It might mean putting to death the dreams you had of your son or daughter becoming a professional athlete and going with him or her to sign up for that art class. It might mean you spend less time parked in front of a TV, inviting your kids to join your thing, and instead, you take that same time and invest it fueling the God-given passions they have. The key is time and doing what *they* want to do—not what *you* want to do.

One of my spiritual heroes is world-renowned apologist Josh McDowell. One of the reasons I appreciate him so much is not because of the man he is on stage or the message he shares in print. It's the man he is behind the scenes.

Back in the early 2000s, Josh had the opportunity to meet President Bush for several minutes after a speech. During their time of interaction, one of Josh's children, Sean, came up to him and said, "Dad, I need you." While the average parent might have brushed off his child, Josh had made a commitment years before that any one of his kids could have his undivided attention at any moment.

So instead of brushing Sean away, he turned to President Bush and stated, "I am sorry, but my child needs my attention." This concluded his conversation with the president. And while some in a position of authority might have seen Josh's actions as impolite, Josh knew where his priorities lay. He was committed to being there for his kids and meeting them at their point of need, regardless the cost.

> The key is time and doing what *they* want to do—not what *you* want to do.

Several days later, Josh received a note from President Bush, thanking him for putting his child first and remarking that it reminded him to call his own children.

This brief story drives home a basic point. In life, there will be many opportunities to brush our kids aside and ask them to meet us on our level. But the heart of the Gospel message calls us to live differently. It calls us to lay aside all of the privileges and rights we feel as parents and go to where our kids are. This is what Jesus did for us. This is what we must do for our gay child.

CHAPTER 4

The Moment I Wanted to Die

In 1997 it felt like I walked into the opportunity of a lifetime. By this point I was 23, had some work experience under my belt, and was open to adventure.

Out of the blue, I received two calls from some friends of mine who told me about a job opening in Bermuda. The job description was broad and simply said, "Personal Executive Assistant to travel the world." All expenses were paid, the monthly salary was good, and the income was tax free. The only requirements listed were that this person had to be Christian, male, and proficient with a computer and typing.

Thinking this was an opportunity to travel I could not refuse, I applied for the job. Almost instantly, the hiring agent thought I was perfect for the position. For the next month, after my 9-5 job at a local printing press in Anaheim, I spent my evenings in training. Compared to all of the technology we have at our disposal today, the process I had to go through seems like a story from the dark ages.

I learned how to use a PC and how to connect remotely using this thing called AOL dial-up internet. I learned how to make international calls from multiple countries using a calling card and discovered how to set up a travel printer to remotely print sales agreements in other countries.

It was crazy. I still remember having to carry this bag of power adapters that allowed me to adapt to whatever country I was in at the time. Such was the picture of a traveling office in 1997.

Prior to this trip, I knew virtually nothing about Bermuda. Sure, I had heard of the Bermuda Triangle, but I knew nothing of the island itself. In May of 1997, my plane touched down, and I found myself in a place that had the most beautiful ocean I had ever witnessed! In all of my travels since that point to places like Maui, Oahu, and West Caribbean Islands, I have never seen water quite as beautiful as the ocean around Bermuda. It was a storybook scene.

A local driver picked me up from the airport, and I loaded all of my belongings into the back of his van. The next few minutes were moments I would never forget. As we drove, I looked out of the window, and what I saw took my breath away. It was as if a graphic artist had colored the sea in an array of colors I had never seen before. I was struck by the dark blue, light blue, aqua, teal, green, clear green, clear, and clear blue colors all pieced together in ways I'd previously thought impossible. It was all I could do to resist the urge to jump out of the slow-moving van and dive into a sea of make-believe.

In a few minutes, we arrived at my apartment. This new home was the converted lower-level basement of a family with two kids. From my bedroom, I could see the south shore. If I stepped outside, I could see the north side of the island. The beaches were a beautiful shade of white, and despite the humidity it felt like a tropical paradise! All I could think to myself at first was, *How does a 23-year-old young man live in such a gorgeous place as this?*

But as great as my initial impressions were, things were about to take a turn for the worse.

A PARADISE TURNED BAD

Statistics show that homosexual men have double the rate of depression and anxiety compared to heterosexual men.[7] And while the last place you might imagine being depressed would be a place like Bermuda, four months into my stay that is exactly where I was.

After moving into my new apartment, it did not take long for reality to set in. From day one, I started working around the clock for a Russian millionaire businessman who had made his fortune in the textile industry. Still in his late 30s, "P" moved his family to Bermuda because it served as an international tax haven for those who wanted to escape paying taxes. Despite his vast wealth, P never flew via private jet. As he explained to me, the reason he always flew commercial was because he found there was safety in numbers. From his perspective, when you flew private, your identity was public to the Russian mafia, and you assumed the greater possibility of being shot out of the sky. That logic was good enough for me, and flying in a private jet suddenly lost its appeal.

For the next few months, I followed P like a little puppy and did my best to please a man who seemed to have it all. Money, drivers, servants, and oceanfront homes were just a few of the many luxuries I witnessed. I was young and wanted to impress the richest man I knew. From what I could see, I estimated he had scores of millions, and through our conversations, I knew it was his goal to amass a fortune of $500M. At that point, he felt he would finally be in position to live comfortably for the rest of his life. Needless to say, our meeting was a clash of lifestyles!

I remember when traveling, P would pull out this wad of $100 bills to cover any expenses I might have. Taking out this massive roll, he would just start counting, pause, and say, "Is this enough?" It always was.

P was an absolute workaholic. It was as if the guy never slept! Trying my best to keep up, I fell right in step with his frantic pace, but it wasn't long until I realized I had exceeded my mental and emotional limitations. Three months of non-stop international travel, and I was done. On one of our overseas trips, I remember being so exhausted that I fell asleep in the front seat of his black German BMW, unable to wake up.

Upon returning to Bermuda, I literally crawled to the shower, reached up to turn on the hot water, and lay on the stall floor for what seemed like an eternity. I could not figure out what was wrong with me. There was no record of depression in my family and no history of mental illness to my knowledge. Instead, I came from a family lineage that said, "Just pick yourself up by your bootstraps."

> "Just pick yourself up by your bootstraps."

It was such a paradox. On one hand, I had it all. The money was great, the travel was fascinating, and the view from my apartment was unparalleled. Still, I knew I had reached my limit, and it was time to quit. I knew I needed help.

Mustering what little strength and courage I had, I loaded myself onto my Vespa moped (the vehicle of choice for non-citizen Bermudans) and motored down to P's office and quit. With that, I said goodbye to the grand opportunity, packed my bags, and flew home to Yorba Linda, California.

I JUST WANT TO DIE

After returning to the U.S., life would not return to normal. My parents were in the midst of a transition and living in an apartment, as they planned to downsize their home.

Little did I know that for the next year I would continue to go through the darkest season of my life. It seemed that not one day could pass without having multiple thoughts of suicide. Sometimes it spooked me how close I came to actually making that decision. All I could think about was ending my life and putting to rest all of the pain I was going through. The thoughts and demonic voices in my head all said the same thing: "Just do it. End it. No one will care. This way you'll be out of your misery." I remember not sleeping all night and then being exhausted throughout the day and still not able to sleep.

On one occasion, I recall having lunch with a youth worker buddy and being fascinated with how he could work, provide, and do the basic tasks of life with ease. At that point, similar responsibilities seemed overwhelming to me, and the thought of life ever returning to normal seemed like a distant fantasy.

It wasn't long before my mom and dad took notice. They could tell something was wrong and became concerned for my health. After multiple heart-wrenching cries with my mom, she finally told my dad, and they agreed I should meet with a psychologist.

At first, this seemed like a great idea, but the moment I stepped through the doors of the clinic, I felt I had made a terrible mistake. In an odd twist of fate, the psychologist I visited turned out to be gay. I knew it from the moment I walked in the door.

I freaked out inside. At that time, only I knew the internal thoughts and attractions I was wrestling with, and here was this man bringing to mind a painful area of my life I wanted very much to avoid. During our sessions, my mind took me to some dark places. Would he take advantage of me? I knew I was in an unhealthy state of mind, and the last thing I needed was a homosexual doctor working with me! My thoughts were so irrational.

As it turned out, this same gay psychologist ended up being the one who provided the clearest pathway out of my depression through the route of the medication known as

Prozac. After using this drug for six-to-eight weeks, something clicked, and my brain felt normal again.

I have never dealt with depression the same way since, and after 12 months of daily doses, I said goodbye to Prozac, and my life returned to a new sense of normalcy.

BACK TO BERMUDA

While I focused on my personal recovery during those four months at home, I spent time working with my uncle in the roofing industry. This was some of the hardest work I'd ever done, but I enjoyed the male comradery and being part of a team.

Each morning, the four of us started the day in prayer, and we challenged each other to grow in our walk with God. But just when things were starting to get back to normal, I received a call from my old boss, P. "Jim, I need you in Bermuda. Would you consider coming back?" *Not a chance!* I thought to myself. Why would I ever go back to a place that gave me such a headache? But P was sincere and promised things would be different this time. There would be less travel and better accommodations.

> This was some of the hardest work I'd ever done, but I enjoyed the male comradery and being part of a team.

And so, with a fresh set of boundaries and expectations in place, I headed back. But this is where things took another turn for the worse and expedited my leap into the gay community.

Because being alone was one of the worst parts of my experience in Bermuda, I invited a friend from church to live with me. He was tall, blonde, and a little on the lazy side of life. "J" was adopted by parents who were well-off and could support him making the trip.

For the next two months, we had a great time, and Bermuda began to live up to what I first envisioned it to be. J would hang out on the beach while I worked in the office. After I got off work, we hung out for several hours and had the time of our lives.

> Words of life can inspire greatness, and words of death can push someone down a dark path.

Then one day, I received a call from P's office, asking me to stop by for a meeting. I knew something was up, and my suspicions were confirmed the moment he shut the door.

"Jim, how many beds are in your apartment?" was his first question.

I froze. "Just the one," I replied. I knew where this was headed.

P sighed and said this was a problem because it gave the appearance to some that I might be gay. As he went on to explain, homosexuality was illegal in Bermuda, and any accusation against *me* could jeopardize *his* financial haven. This was not a risk he was willing to take, and the only solution was to release me from my position.

So, for a second time in just a few months, I found myself unemployed.

Walking out of that office, I was devastated. Not only did J and I not have that kind of relationship, but my record prior to this point was spotless. Not once had I ever acted out with a member of the same sex, either in Bermuda or in the U.S. Now, here I was accused of a "crime" I had never committed.

As is too often the case, human beings live up to who they are told they are. Words of life can inspire greatness, and words of death can push someone down a dark path.

While I do not blame P for my decision to eventually come out as gay, it was this bitter interaction that broke my resistance. For nearly 15 years, I had opposed any urge to act on my same-sex desires, but this wave of shame and embarrassment pushed me over the edge. If people like P saw me as gay, maybe I was that way after all. Why should I resist being whom everyone else already thought I was? Maybe I was the mistake everyone seemed to think I was.

> Every person alive today lives in the tension between a world that is broken and the truth that God is good.

After I returned home, I spent a month in Newport Beach and made plans to move to the gay-friendly city of Portland. My time in the closet was coming to a close.

WHY DOES GOD ALLOW HIS CHILDREN TO LAMENT?

This experience and others have led me to ask a very basic question: *Why does God allow His created beings to go through seasons of despair?*

Scripture is filled with lament. There is even an entire book of the Bible named Lamentations. In his book *Dark Clouds, Deep Mercy*, Mark Vroegop notes, "Lament is the honest cry of a hurting heart wrestling with the paradox of pain and the promise of God's goodness."[8]

Every person alive today lives in the tension between a world that is broken and the truth that God is good. And despite most people's desire to live the good life and get through as best they can without pain and suffering, God chooses to allow His created beings to go through some dark nights of the soul.

I say this because there were many times I pleaded with God to take away my same-sex attraction. I hated it because it felt like this attraction was a large impediment that blocked my ability to love and be loved.

The whole concept of living in a state of prolonged suffering feels so unjust. Yet when I look back on the history of the Christian faith, I cannot help but observe a trend that those who were often the closest to God experienced some of the greatest degrees of suffering. It might be for this reason that author Jen Pollock Michel writes, "For all its seemingly impolitic, impious qualities, lament is a confession of faith."[9]

Think about it. Almost all of the twelve disciples lost their lives because they had chosen to place their identity in Christ. Most individuals in the churches the Apostle Paul addressed in his letters were those who had faced severe persecution, many times resulting in the loss of property, possessions, or sometimes life itself.

> I cannot help but observe a trend that those who were often the closest to God experienced some of the greatest degrees of suffering.

Laying these illustrations aside, I find myself worshiping a God who gave His very Son to die on a cross. No amount of spin can take away the horrible pain Christ endured when He took on Himself the physical weight of nails piercing His skin and the spiritual weight of humanity's sin.

Suffering in and of itself is not good. But there is much good that can come out of times of suffering—good that many in our world fail to see.

My Catholic friends understand this much better than evangelicals in the western world. Their crucifix resembles Jesus on the cross in a point of anguish, suffering, and pain, and the message is clear—Jesus died for our sins, and by his wounds we are healed. However, western evangelicals struggle to embrace this concept and have a hard time focusing on the suffering of Christ. The result is that we have developed an incomplete perspective of what God is doing in the midst of our darkest hours of pain.

When I was in seminary several years ago, I began reading Psalm 77 as part of my Biblical Interpretation class. The professor was Dr. John Hartley, one of the best teachers I have ever heard. He felt that by studying this passage, we would have a better understanding of pain and suffering. He was not mistaken.

> We have developed an incomplete perspective of what God is doing in the midst of our darkest hours of pain.

This psalm is short but powerful. It starts off on a somber note with the psalmist lamenting the fact that he has spent his night crying out to God for help. He is groaning and growing faint because the weight he carries is so heavy. And as disheartening as these initial words might seem to some, they offered hope to me. Through them, I saw the pain and suffering so many people in this world, including myself, had experienced. I realized that God wants us to bring our pain and troubles to him.

Psalm 77 forever changed the way I read the Bible, and it got me through some pretty dark days.

TWO THOUGHTS

If you are reading this as a mom or dad of a gay son, it's quite possible you find yourself in your own season of lament. But it's in this moment that I would encourage you to do two things.

First, acknowledge the pain of your child. Despite what you might see, there is pain he carries. I promise you that the hardened image he might display when you get together does not tell the full story. Deep down, there is hurt, fear, and anger you do not see.

> Deep down, there is hurt, fear, and anger you do not see.

Second, lean into the arms of God. The privilege of having a relationship with our Heavenly Father is that He invites us to bring our burdens to Him. Take full advantage of this. Use this season of lament as an opportunity to strengthen your prayer life.

And as you learn to lament well, you will develop God's heart for yourself and your gay child.

Part 2

Mistaken Love

CHAPTER 5

Coming Out

I couldn't wait to have sex. After years of resistance, I was ready to step out and express my love for others any way I chose. I wanted to love and be loved.

My coming out started on the southwest side of Portland in 1997. SW Stark Street was an area of the city where all the gay bars were located. It has since been renamed to Harvey Milk Street in 2017 in honor of California's first openly gay elected official.

Borrowing my best friend Chris' black Nissan pickup truck, I nervously drove into this community, parking by the LGBTQ-friendly restaurant called Hamburger Mary's. At this point, I was still a virgin, and this new lifestyle was out of my comfort zone. To my dissatisfaction, nothing happened that night or the next four consecutive nights I returned. My resistance levels were gone, but the true love I sought seemed evasive.

> **I wanted to love and be loved.**

Finally, I turned to the online world and ended up hooking up with a man who was a United Airlines flight attendant. After speaking on the phone, "O" flew to Portland to meet me.

I told him I was a virgin, and from there, we had a brief encounter that was based on nothing more than erotic desire. Like every relationship I had experienced with members of the *opposite* sex, this new relationship turned out to be equally anticlimactic. Because O lived in another state and our relationship was nothing more than a sexual attraction, it soon fell apart. [Side Note: Several decades later, O reached out to me and said he had become a Christian. For that, I am grateful.]

> I think this desire only highlighted the real need in my life, a need to be connected to my dad and other healthy heterosexual males.

Over the next two years, I moved from one partner to the next. Personally, I was more attracted to men who were older. And looking back, I think this desire only highlighted the real need in my life—a need to be connected to my dad and other healthy heterosexual males.

SIN IS FUN

While I have heard some Christians speak about sinful lifestyles as horrible, unhappy states of existence, the truth for me was that sin was a lot of fun.

It was thrilling to have sex with multiple partners whenever I chose. Ever since becoming aware of my homoerotic desires as a kid, I had kept my guard up and said no to whatever impulses I had. Now, I was free to do as I always wanted, and my actions were seen as normal by those around me.

Because the gay community I hung out in was mostly made up of males with strong sexual desires, finding someone to have sex with was seldom a problem. And aside from those first few awkward days, it didn't matter where I was; there was always another guy who wanted what I wanted—a quick sexual fix.

While many straight males I knew actually paid money to hire a prostitute, it always struck me as odd. In my mind, who would need to do that? Why would you pay to have sex with someone when you could be gay and get it for free?!

That said, while there was some short-term fulfillment in these sexual one-offs, I noticed that each new sexual encounter seemed to do less to fill the longing I had. As Sam Allberry so accurately notes, "Sexuality is a little like a post-it note. The first time you use it, it sticks well. But when it is reapplied too many times, it loses its capacity to stick to anything. We are simply not designed for multiple sexual relationships. Sex becomes less relational, more functional and less satisfying as a result. Casual sexual encounters are made to look harmless and fun in most sitcoms, but the consequences in real life are far more serious—emptiness, brokenness and devastation."[10] That was my story.

Sometimes I chuckle to myself when I listen to the words of my gay friends who are still active in the lifestyle because their language always revolves around sex. I remember my buddy "R" (a former gay man who has since come to Christ) saying to me, "You know, Jim, it's all about worshipping the penis." Crude as that sounded, I found his assessment accurate because it reflected many of the relationships I witnessed as well as my own personal experience. During my five years in the gay community, my entire identity revolved around fulfilling my sexual desires. It took me years to get away from that.

To this point, I remember having a conversation with my dad after I stepped away from the homosexual lifestyle. We were watching TV, and I couldn't help but point out everything the way I saw it. "They're queer," "She's a dyke," and "He's gay," I remarked. Finally, he had enough. "Stop it!" he snapped. "You label everything as sexual. Can't you just accept things for what they are?"

I realized he was right. I did see the world primarily through the lens of sexual identity. That was how I discovered value, and that was how I subconsciously evaluated others. I was this young man who had never experienced what it felt like to have a healthy male bonding experience. My wires were crossed, and I had this deep hunger to connect with someone. I thought having sex with more men would meet this itch, but my wounds only continued to get deeper. In fact, the more sex I had, the larger this void in my life grew.

All of it brought me back to this fundamental truth: sin is a fun up-front investment, but the returns greatly diminish over time.

THE UGLY SIDE

The more I interacted with members in the LGBTQ community, the more my heart continued to hurt for the immense brokenness I witnessed.

Yes, there were still thrills, but there were also stories of intense heartbreak. For instance, I remember sitting in a gay bar off a street in downtown Portland when I happened to meet a man who was wearing a dress. His name was Mary.

A hermaphrodite from birth, Mary possessed both male and female chromosomes—a true transgender. I remember looking at the ultrasound pictures Mary showed me of her female and male genitalia. I was shocked and had never encountered someone like her before.

Mary shared of how when she was younger, her feminine qualities were the predominant features on display. But as she aged, the testosterone kicked in, and her Adam's apple became noticeable. As you might imagine, Mary suffered no end of bullying among her peers. Who was she? What was her real identity? How could she find someone to love and accept her for who she was when she was not even sure herself?

Listening to stories like Mary's revealed the vast gap that existed between the world I was living in and the church community I had been raised in as a child. In the back of my mind, I told myself that if I ever went back to the church, I would make it my life's mission to help others who had gone through situations like Mary's.

MY FIRST MALE RELATIONSHIP

All of the ugliness and unfulfillment I experienced during my first few dating relationships led me to think that a committed monogamous relationship was what I needed. This started when I met my first partner, "R."

The year was 1999, and it was a point in history when AOL chat rooms were a thing. After a brief online conversation, we decided to meet up, and I drove from Anaheim Hills to his home in Palm Springs. He made dinner and served wine, and I remember thinking the entire evening was so romantic and beautiful.

R was tall, dark, and handsome with good hair and a thin build. He spent most of his days as an artist or surfing on the beach. Because I preferred men who were older, I did not mind the 14-year age gap. At 37, he was more established, and his home was nothing short of impressive. He happened to be only a few doors down from where the famous actress Lucille Ball used to live.

Over dinner, R told me his house used to be part of Hugh Hefner's (the founder of *Playboy*) estate until it was divided up and sold as individual residences. The layout of the home was fabulous, and it was as if the exterior and interior of the home were one. The gray and blue stone that lined the flooring of the home extended into the backyard and both in and around the pool.

The property had a gate and was surrounded by trees that served as a privacy screen. After we decided to start seeing each other, I remember going over to his house and swimming naked with R in the backyard pool. In my mind, I finally had it all. I had found true love, could be myself, and was seemingly with someone who had a lot of money to spare!

But there was a catch.

Prior to ever having sex, R sat me down and told me the tough news—he was HIV positive. I didn't care. I placed my hand on his and said, "I'm okay with that." He wasn't done and continued by telling me he was Hepatitis C positive as well and that I should never touch his blood. This was also a tertiary point in my mind, and my desire for love clouded what little judgment I had.

> My desire for love clouded what little judgment I had.

For three months, our relationship was strong, but then I called it off. The pressures I felt from my family were strong, and I wasn't sure this partnership was the best fit. The decision broke both our hearts.

But after the fourth of July weekend following our breakup, I changed my mind. I drove up to Palm Springs, only to discover R had sold his home and was now living in his art gallery. He was ecstatic and invited me to join him, so I moved what little belongings I had into the store. This was where we would live for months until we sold enough art to rent a home in the exclusive Vista Las Palmas (micro estates) adjacent to Las Palmas (macro estates) in North Palm Springs.

This home was almost as amazing as R's previous place, and for the next few years, I had the time of my life. It's kind of embarrassing when I think back to it. We no longer lived in a community that was as private, and there was a neighbor lady whose house overlooked our back yard. I can only imagine her thoughts when she saw R and me sunbathing in the nude!

It was wild and crazy, but I was in love.

"JIM, DO YOU STILL READ YOUR BIBLE?"

During my five years in the gay community, only two of my Christian friends continued to reach out. Chris and Michelle were amazing, and my change in lifestyle did not put an end to our relationship. When I sensed my life was heading in a new direction, I reached out and asked them to start praying. "I'm still gay," I reminded them, "but I want your prayers." One time, I remember Michelle giving me a call, and in the midst our conversation she asked me what I considered to be a bizarre question: "Jim, do you still read your Bible?"

"Of course not," I shot back. "Why should I?" And then I softened and gave a more reflective response. "Michelle, the reason I don't read the Bible is because I am afraid it will change me." My own words shocked even me, and I realized something about myself. I was comfortable keeping a Bible on top of the fireplace in our home because this told others I was a Christian. But I was fearful of what might happen if I cracked open the pages.

> I don't read the Bible—because I am afraid it will change me.

It might seem odd, but the entire time I was with R, I found myself attempting to apply Christian principles to our relationship. We both did in a way. R wasn't Christian, but he believed God existed, as most artists do. I think he thought the restraints of the Christian God were too heavy and preferred to paint the portrait of his life with a broader brush. It's as if he wanted a blank canvas to paint God in his image. Jesus was not enough.

On one hand, we were committed to one another, but on the other hand, we were fine inviting others into our relationship. I recalled coming back to our home one time and seeing R having sex with another man. While this was "permissible" under our agreement with each other, I couldn't help but feel jealous. It was all very strange. While in some respects we were committed to each other, in others we wanted to experience all of the extended benefits

> Much as I had a disconnect with my physical father, I had a disconnect with my spiritual Father.

life had to offer. When we went to a bar, we often tried to bring someone else home to share the bed. Again, it was this awkward dance of living a "moral life" but wanting to do it on our terms. It was a "Jesus plus" lifestyle.

My greatest problem at this point was that I thought of Jesus as my Savior and not as my Lord. I loved the security and sense of peace that believing in God brought, but I had little interest in living life according to His direction.

Much as I had a disconnect with my physical father, I had a disconnect with my spiritual Father. Just as I could never replace the gap I sensed with my earthly dad, I realized there was no amount of connection with others that could ever replace the void I felt with my Heavenly Father. My satisfaction in God was low, and this meant I needed to search out happiness in areas that were contrary to his plan.

FULL-BLOWN NARCISSIST

For many in the gay community, sexuality is the most important part of their life which develops an unhealthy sense of narcissism.

Fast forward a few years to when I had gotten my life together and I was sitting with my family around a Christmas tree in Austin, Texas. I shared with them that I had met a girl named Amanda and would be proposing to her.

My sister's immediate reply was, "Does Amanda know how selfish you are?" And as I look back on my life from my sister's perspective, she had good reason to worry because those five years as a gay man were lived as a life consumed with self.

Sometimes I grimace in pain when I think back on some of my actions. Take my brother's wedding for example. When Jeff was getting married, he asked me to be his best man. This was probably more of an act of love than it was preference. Despite growing up together, our life journeys had taken us in very different directions.

> Sexuality is the most important part of their life which develops an unhealthy sense of narcissism.

Saying yes, I boarded a plane from Palm Springs to Austin. But when I got to Dallas, I had a sudden burst of inspiration. Rather than completing the final leg of the journey to Austin, I exited the DFW airport, picked out a rental car, and turned the three-hour drive into a mini road trip so I could check out the sites.

The only problem was that I didn't tell my brother. Several hours later, Jeff gave me a call: "Hey, I see your bags at the airport, but I don't see you. Where are you?"

Rather than issuing an apology, I instructed him to pick up my bags and take them to his home, and I would be there later. I can only imagine what he muttered to himself when I hung up the phone.

When I finally did arrive at his wedding, I was thoroughly self-consumed. To make matters worse, one of my brother's best friends—who probably should have been his best man—let me borrow his car. I had returned my rental and needed some way to get around. Without giving it a second thought,

> My actions and reactions to events were motivated out of envy and bitterness.

I accepted his offer, got in the car, and lit up a cigarette. I cared little about what he might think to have a car smelling like smoke returned to him.

Even though I was not the one getting married, you might have thought I was by my actions. Everything I did revolved around me, and I made it a point to show I had no desire to be there and wanted little to do with any of those involved in both wedding parties.

It wasn't as if I went to Austin with the intended goal of wreaking havoc, but my actions and reactions to events were motivated out of envy and bitterness. For example, I remember someone videotaping the rehearsal, and when they turned the shot to me, I flipped off the camera during my turn to comment. I was a total jerk.

My sister's wedding was not much better. Prior to her big day, I dyed my eyebrows jet black. They looked hideous, and my sister was understandably upset. Even now, she still declares I ruined her wedding photos, and whenever my wife Amanda sees the photo of me with my two siblings, she cannot believe that one of those people is actually me!

WHAT WAS GOING ON?

When I look back on this period of my life, it is obvious to me why I reacted the way I did. I was angry at my siblings for having what I could not have. It bothered me that they now had a marriage that made my parents proud and that they would experience the excitement of raising a family in a way I never would. I was the misfit, the mistake. They were the special ones.

To you parents who are going through the journey of a son responding the way I did, hold on, take a deep breath, and try to see the bigger picture. Your child is hurt in ways you might not be able to see, and his expression of this hurt might come in ways that are very painful to bear.

It does not justify or excuse his behavior, but it does offer some explanation and should shift the way you respond. Instead of attacking him at every turn and falling into his game of back-and-forth accusations, pull back, collect your thoughts, and regroup. Commit yourself to the arms of Jesus and lean in tighter to Him. It is only as you do this will you have the love you need for your child.

> Your child is hurt in ways you might not be able to see, and his expression of this hurt might come in ways that are very painful to bear.

CHAPTER 6

Broke and Kicked to the Curb

"I didn't marry a woman," R screamed at me. The date was June 8, 2002, and for months leading up to this argument, we exchanged verbal blows. How much of this was tied to personality differences and how much to R's addiction to alcohol and marijuana I'll never know. All I knew was that our disagreements continued to worsen by the day.

There were days he went insane. One time, we were driving from Palm Springs to Orange County when his screams and emotional abuse grew so intense I demanded he pull the car over and let me out. I think at that point he realized he had gone too far because, as he pulled the car to the side of the interstate, he tried to apologize. But I was having none of it and got out, called one of my friends, and asked her to pick me up.

Even though gay marriage was not legal at the time, R and I both wore wedding rings and acted like we were married. Neither one of us took on the male or female roles, and we saw our relationship as a mutual balance of power. R was an artist, and I ran the operational side of our business.

Together, we owned this nice little art gallery in a high-end area of Palm Springs. I still remember the terracotta-colored brick walls on the outside along with the white stucco on the interior. We were located right next to a busy intersection, making it easy for passersby to walk in and view what we had on display.

What helped our business, we were situated beside a prominent hairdresser named T. Allan King. He was a legend in his industry, and the bottom price for haircuts started around $150-$250. Needless to say, the cliental he brought into his shop were people who had some serious cash. Clients like Sally Nordstrom—former wife of John Nordstrom, the founder of the Nordstrom Department stores. Before their appointments, customers of King's would often stop by our store and browse what we had on display.

> **People in Al-Anon are often sicker than actual alcoholics.**

On one occasion, one of these clients came in, and we started talking. I was 28 at the time, and she was probably in her mid-60s. I forget how we got on the subject, but we began chatting about what was going on in my life, and she mentioned a program called Al-Anon, a self-help support group for people dealing with alcoholics.

I had heard of AA (Alcoholics Anonymous), but Al-Anon was the reverse of this program. It was and is for people who *live* with an alcoholic. Strange as it might seem, I would argue that people in Al-Anon are often sicker than actual alcoholics. After going to several meetings, I listened to some of the horror stories people shared and thought to myself, *These people are nuts! How do they stay in these abusive relationships? Why don't they leave?!*

But then I began to evaluate my own situation with R. I realized that all the while I expressed my own shock at people who would not leave their hard situations, I was continuing to remain in my own abusive relationship. And for the first time in my life, I started to gain a small understanding of the term "battered spouse syndrome." I could understand how people who were suffering abuse could continue to go back to their abuser—because I was doing the exact same thing!

Prior to that point, neither R nor I played the effeminate role in our relationship, and R was not about to let that start. After returning home from my sister's wedding, I pulled into our home in Vista Las Palmas. Keep in mind that my eyebrows were still dyed jet black. This prompted him to make the snarky remark, "I didn't marry a woman!" I can't remember what I said back to him, but it probably wasn't nice.

"Get out! Get out!" he screamed, his level of anger reaching a new height I had not previously witnessed.

"Gladly," I snapped. Knowing this situation could get bad pretty fast, I picked up the phone to call the cops. I was beyond reconciling this relationship and only wanted to grab my things and move out. Little did I know that even in that moment, God was working in the background of my life.

The scales had finally come off my eyes, and I saw the life I was choosing to live. Thankfully, I met a gay man who had just bought and restored the apartment complex across the street from one of our art galleries. Out of the goodness of his heart, he offered to let me stay rent-free in one of their apartments for one month so that I could get my feet under me again.

So on that day, I moved out from R for good.

THE UNSEEN HAND OF GOD

I recall chatting with one of my Palm Springs' police officer friends, and she remarked that the worst domestic disputes she ever encountered were between homosexuals and lesbians. Living in the community as long as I did, I stand behind her assessment. These disputes are awful.

Soon after I called, two police officers arrived at our door and knocked. I didn't know it then, but both of them turned out to be Christians.

Late that evening, I drove over to my new two-story apartment mini complex. It was an old building that dated back to the early twentieth century. It had a red-tiled floor with a wooden beam ceiling. The apartment building was surrounded by a white-walled fence that was 8-10 feet high.

> God, I'm yours again.

Within this fencing was a big Spanish-style gate you had to enter to get inside and a red terracotta-sided swimming pool in the center of the oasis. It felt like a fortress, and that was exactly what I needed at the moment.

I plopped down on the floor and stared up at the vaulted ceiling. I had no belongings, no electricity, no air conditioning, and no money. It was June 8, 2002, and in the summer in Palm Springs, it's hotter than you can imagine. As I lay there with beads of sweat dripping from my forehead, I looked up, and the only words that came to mind were, "God, I'm yours again."

At the time, I meant this with some conditions. I could not deny that God was at work in my life. The handwriting was on the wall. But it was still my goal to get on my feet and re-enter the exact same lifestyle—this time with a different partner who would show me genuine love. That was my goal, but God had different plans.

EVERYTHING TO NOTHING

After R and I broke up, my net worth was reduced to zero. Because I trusted him, I naively agreed to a joint bank account. The day we fought, R withdrew all of the money we had in the account and moved it to another one that bore only his name. In addition, he wiped my name off the business. I had no cash on hand and did not have a dime to my name. It was a sad picture. Here I was, a 28-year-old man who had started two companies, had a home, and was now reduced to nothing.

It's not as if R and I were multimillionaires. Even though we would take in upwards of $200,000 a year, we somehow always found a way to spend more than we made. In the art business, it's often feast or famine. Some months you might make $30,000 in sales and the next month almost nothing. For example, just prior to 9/11, we were on pace for the greatest season we had ever had.

Our business was featured on the cover of Palm Springs Magazine Annual Edition, and we were in every hotel room in the area for the year! This magazine released in August, and people started coming to our store from all over the region. Business was incredible!

But, soon after 9/11 happened, everything dried up, and we went from record sales to zero sales for the remainder of the year. As you might imagine, this only contributed to R's alcohol addiction and heightened our disagreements. We were on the path to financial ruin.

Even though my personal financial loss was minimal when R chose to cut me out of the equation, I was still in a powerless position. I had only debt on my credit card, no cash, and no access to customer payments. Even though I could have gone to court and technically fought for what was mine, my friend advised me to let it go. I took her advice.

The next morning after I left R, I slid open the old rustic-style barn door to my apartment and stepped outside. Looking out at the courtyard area that served as grand central station for the 14 private apartment residents, I felt stuck.

"Lord, what am I going to do?" I wondered. Having no money meant my options were limited. But looking down at my keyring, I remembered I had a membership to Gold's Gym, so I strolled out the front gate to jump in my 1997

Acura RL. As I did, I looked down on the sidewalk and saw a $5 bill lying on the ground.

In that moment, God spoke to me and said, "Jim, I took care of the Israelites in the desert, and I will take care of you in yours." I can promise you that $5 had never meant so much before nor has it since.

At the time, Denny's restaurant had a Grand Slam Breakfast promotion for $2.99. And thanks to that $5 bill, this got me a plate of pancakes and eggs and left just enough for a tip!

It's hard to describe the excitement I experienced that day. Sometimes I look at new converts to Christ, and I see how happy and joyful they are. I can say that when you sense God at work in your life, there is a joy that comes over you that cannot help but be expressed.

After eating at Denny's, I called the manager over and started sharing all that God had done for me. I'm pretty sure he thought I was crazy, and there is a part of me that couldn't blame him! From an external perspective, I didn't have much reason to be thankful. I had just lost everything, yet I felt happier than I had in years.

BAD TO WORSE

Within 24 hours, R falsified a police report and said I was violent, had guns, and was going to harm him. Anyone who knew me during this time would have realized how laughable this suggestion was. I wasn't an angel by any stretch of the imagination, but I certainly wasn't the devil.

Before I knew it, there was a Palm Springs police officer at my door, issuing me a temporary restraining order. The irony I felt in this moment could hardly be overstated. Here I was, the son of a Los Angeles sheriff's deputy with zero history of any violence, being served with a restraining order.

I was shocked and didn't know what to say. But even in that moment, I witnessed the hand of God. The police officer who issued the warrant was someone I recognized. Being the talkative person I have always been, I opened up to her and started telling her that what I was doing was sin. It's hard to know what she was thinking while she kept quiet and listened. This police officer's name was Merritt, and I would find out later that she, like her two previous counterparts, was a Christian.

> If I would not have lost it all, I know I would have kept going down the same path.

This connection still amazes me. When the typical police officer goes out on a 415 domestic call, I'm not sure how many of them become friends with their suspect in question, but I will venture to guess the number is not high. Merrit was the exception, and we soon became friends.

At my darkest moment, God showed me He still cared and was present. He would not allow evil to destroy me. The day that temporary restraining order went into effect, I was banned from going near our home in Vista Las Palmas or our art galleries. This was a bit of a problem seeing as though my apartment was less than a thousand feet from our store. Afraid I wouldn't even be able to leave my home and worried about the mark this restraint would leave on my record, I went to court. R never showed, so thankfully, the charges were dismissed and expunged. My attorney and even the judge saw it as a falsified report.

Losing everything was terrible in the moment. But looking back it turned out to be a great blessing. If I would not have lost it all, I know I would have kept going down the same path.

A LIFE-CHANGING TRIP TO PENNSYLVANIA

Out of the blue, one of my best friends from college reached out to me. He lived with his wife and kids in Portland, Oregon. He invited me to fly and meet them in Williamsburg, Pennsylvania (Little League capital of the world) so I could spend a few weeks with them.

Needing any sort of diversion I could find, I borrowed money from my parents and caught the next plane to Pennsylvania. Stepping out of the Williamsburg airport, I was a sight most people in that community were unaccustomed to seeing.

> The joy of hearing Scripture taught each week did wonders for my soul.

"Is that makeup on Jim's face?" Chris' wife asked him. It wasn't makeup but dyed hair and dyed eye lashes and brows. Let's just say I was not viewed as the manliest man in Williamsburg that day!

The next few weeks were a whirlwind of activity but an oasis of peace. It was amazing what getting out of the city and being in nature did for me. I stayed with Chris' uncle and worked for the Smith family on their farm all day, doing tasks I had only read about in books. From bailing hay to chopping wood, the hard physical labor set my mind at ease. I felt cleansed.

Aside from two funerals, I hadn't been in church for five years. However, I started attending this small Baptist congregation in the town of Mooreland, Pennsylvania, and my life began to change. The joy of hearing Scripture taught each week did wonders for my soul.

After three weeks, I flew back to Palm Springs, and my friend who had loaned me the apartment said I needed to make a decision. I needed to start paying rent, or I needed to move out. Fair enough. Still, I had almost no money to my name.

My parents said I could move in with them, but that was the last place I wanted to go. However, by this point, I was out of options. It was time to go home.

CHAPTER 7

My Real Struggle with Identity

The emotions I experienced in those days after leaving R were amazing. Released from the verbal and emotional abuse, I felt like a brand-new person.

That said, while I experienced freedom, I did not know which direction to turn. Should I head back to the gay community and live as I had lived before with a new partner, or was God getting ahold of my heart? There were all of these God moments I could not deny. It might be someone loaning me $100 to cover an electrical bill, buying me a meal, or saying a kind word. I hated what I was going through, but even before this season came about, I knew God was working. I knew He had been active in my life for a while.

Flash back a few months prior to my breakup with R, and I sensed God's presence in a very unusual way. R and I were in the midst of verbal argument in our dining room. During this heated verbal exchange, I sensed God say that one day I would publicly share my story with others. The moment was so intense that I actually lifted my head toward the ceiling and thought to myself, *What was that?!*

Looking back, I can see how God was working even in the midst of my most painful moments in the gay community. It all came together the day I stepped away. It was then I discovered how much God loved me and how badly Satan wanted me back in chains.

THE WAR FOR MY SOUL

As soon as I breathed those words, "God, I'm yours again," I could tell there was a ravenous war for my soul. Demonic attacks began to occur, and I started having nightmares. As I began to find my way back to God, there were moments I could not deny His movement that were followed by times of intense temptation to get right back into my previous lifestyle.

> There was a ravenous war for my soul.

When I made the decision to move back in with my parents, I had a bi-sexual buddy named Aaron who volunteered to give me a hand. After several of my neighbors helped us load my things, we drove the U-Haul from my apartment in Palm Springs to my parents' home in Yorba Linda.

Aaron was someone who had been diagnosed with a brain tumor but had experienced a strong recovery. I remember the times I would visit him in Palm Springs General Hospital and help with some of the most basic tasks like giving his face a shave. Through this unique experience, we bonded and became closer friends.

I suppose both of us knew there was some attraction we held for each other, even though it did not build into anything. When I moved back in with my parents, I suddenly felt this urge to act out and take this relationship in a sexual direction. My parents were out of town when we pulled in their driveway, and I thought it would be an opportune moment to act on my desires.

But it was here I sensed the tension of God's grace. On one hand, I felt the tug to return to my past, but on the other hand, I experienced new supernatural strength. Instead of taking our relationship in a sexual direction, I said goodbye to Aaron and finished unpacking my stuff in my parents' new home in Vista Del Verde.

I was stepping into grace, but I was saying goodbye to a world I did not want to leave.

NOT A BAD PERSON

Part of my problem coming back to God was that I did not see myself as a bad person. I was always the good guy. My parents were Catholic when I was a baby, so I was baptized into the church as an infant. This meant I had "fire insurance," but it said nothing about my relationship with Christ. Even though I technically accepted Christ when I was four and then again when I was seven, something was missing—even if no one else could see.

All throughout my growing up years, I was known as the good guy. When I was in eighth grade, I won a Christian service award as the top student who lived like Jesus. It was the highest honor you could receive when you graduated. Only one person in the eighth-grade graduating class received this award.

The worst "sins" I ever committed were during my years at Troy High School in Fullerton, California. During finals when I was a sophomore, members of our class were called on to give an oral report for our final reading project. Each student selected different classical pieces of literature, submitted a written report, and spoke during class in one of the time slots available over the next two weeks. I volunteered to go first and get mine out of the way. After I did so, I pulled aside a friend of mine and told her we should skip class and go down to the local coffee shop and get a donut.

Little did I know the school had an automated calling system in place if anyone ever missed a class. When I returned home that evening, my parents knew what I had done. I was mortified and grounded!

Another time I committed an act of rebellion was when I went mudding with my parents' white Jeep. My dad had told me numerous times to never drive the Jeep into a mud pit, but there was a day I just couldn't resist. After a good hard rain one afternoon, my buddy and I pulled off the freeway and spent the next hour mud-romping through a field that looked more like a swamp. Realizing we needed to cover our tracks, we took the Jeep to a car wash and scrubbed it from top to bottom.

> I'm sure God gives parents a heightened sense of discernment.

I'm sure God gives parents a heightened sense of discernment, because it wasn't minutes after I got home that Dad called me out to look at the car. He noticed a bit of mud under the car on the garage floor and wanted to know what had happened. I told him and went on restriction once again.

This was the depth of my career as a seasoned criminal. I was the kid that never did anything wrong, was ashamed if I ever did, and was the most likely to rat out one of my friends if they ever broke the rules. I was respectful, kind, and decent. I was a good person, and I thought that was enough.

MY BAD THEOLOGY

While I didn't know it at the time, I had adopted a faulty theological framework and viewed my relation to God and passion for sin from a dysfunctional perspective. After serving for 17 years as a pastor and earning a Master of Divinity from Azusa Pacific University, I can look back and say my view of sin was pretty messed up.

To my gay friends, I was a puzzlement. When I was still with R, they would sometimes ask me, "Jim, how can you be part of the gay community and still profess to be a Christian?"

"Easy," I responded. "I'm just forgiven." I had the Christian tag, the fire insurance that would keep me out of hell, and a loving God who would forgive any sins I might commit.

For me, I viewed being gay as a way to enhance my life and fill a void I could not fill otherwise. But in the words of my friend Joe Dallas, "Satan's strategy in leading humans astray, whether the arena is doctrinal or moral, is to deceive an individual into thinking that what God has forbidden is not really wrong or destructive but rather is life-enhancing."[11] Yes or no? Did God really say that?

While I bought into this "forgiven sinner paradigm," I discounted the words of the Apostle Paul in Romans 6:1-2, "What shall we say, then? Shall we go on sinning so that grace may increase? By no means! We are those who have died to sin; how can we live in it any longer?" As many commentators note, Paul might as well be shouting these words, "By no means!"

> Satan's strategy in leading humans astray, whether the arena is doctrinal or moral, is to deceive an individual into thinking that what God has forbidden is not really wrong or destructive but rather is life-enhancing.

I think the reason he comes down so strong on this position is because past and present human beings struggle to grasp this concept. We just cannot seem to escape this "Jesus plus" mindset. We want to keep Him around in our lives but also want the message of the gospel to adapt to our standard of living. It's Jesus plus a same-sex partnership; Jesus plus adultery; Jesus plus sin.

But as Sam Allberry notes, "If someone thinks the gospel has somehow slotted into their life quite easily, without causing any major adjustments to their lifestyle or aspirations, it is likely that they have not really started following Jesus at all."[12]

Despite any statements I made to the contrary, all the while I spoke of being a Christian, my life showed no evidence of fruit. I knew what I was doing was wrong, and I had an underlying moral compass. I felt like a modern-day Jonah who could not escape God's call on my life. No matter where I went, I continued to sense the presence

> I was the one who was running from Him— all the while He was running for me.

of God. If I flew to an expo in Germany and participated in bathhouse activities, God was there. When R and I booked reservations in Maui and went to gay bars, God was there.

I was the one who was running from Him—all the while He was running for me.

IDENTITY IN CHRIST

After I returned home, the next few years were filled with opportunities to go back to the lifestyle I had left behind. One of my greatest fears coming back to the Lord was that I would fall sexually. Part of this was healthy because it taught me to be humble and depend on God for strength. It is because of His goodness that I have not acted out sexually with another man since my return to Christ in 2002.

Just this statement might cause some skeptics to say, "Jim, aren't you living a lie? How can you have a wife and kids when you sometimes have thoughts about sex with men?"

It is here I need to pause and offer some pushback. When I was an active participant in the gay community, that became my primary identity. Every question of my being pointed back to the simple statement, "I, Jim Domen, am gay."

When I started to make my way back to Jesus, this changed, and Christ became my primary identity. Quoting from Allberry again, he couldn't be more right when he states, "I first began to properly understand something of my sexuality around the same time that I began to understand Jesus Christ."[13] The two are interconnected!

Our society gets the idea of finding identity. "I am a fashionista," "I am an athlete," or "I am an American." These are all titles we understand. But when it comes to the Christian life, the phrase "I am a Christian" seems ambiguous.

To many, it feels wrong to compare it to any other form of identity such as someone's race or sex. We get why it's wrong to use some form of a racial slur, but we have little problem using a phrase like, "Oh my God" or other phrases that use God's name in vain. Why? It's because we have prioritized one over the other. *One is real, and the other is just a belief* is what we tell ourselves.

> Our greatest identity in life does not come from sexual orientation, sex, or racial background. It comes from connection to our Creator.

But this could not be more inaccurate. Our greatest identity in life does not come from sexual orientation, sex, or racial background. It comes from connection to our Creator. This is where all true identity begins, and anything that does not start there falls short and results in a life filled with unfulfillment.

In the words of Jackie Hill Perry, "The only constant in this world is God. Gayness, on the other hand, can be an immovable identity only when the heart is unwilling to bow."[14] Christopher Yuan seconds this statement, "My sexual orientation didn't have to be the core of who I was. My primary identity didn't have to be defined by my feelings or sexual attractions. My identity was not 'gay' or 'homosexual,' or even 'heterosexual,' for that matter. But my identity as a child of the living God must be in Jesus Christ alone."[15]

Only as I began to understand my identity in Christ did I begin to properly understand how to view my identity as a heterosexual who can be tempted by same-sex attraction.

CHAPTER 8

Re-Adjusting to a Different World

When my parents returned home and found me there, they knew I had come back for good. My dad couldn't help but think back to the parable of the Prodigal Son in Luke 15 and how the dad killed the fattened calf for his youngest child who returned home.

This prompted him to turn to me and say, "Jim, I don't have a herd of cattle to kill a fattened calf, but I *can* take you to the nicest steak house I know." That night, he and my mom drove me to this high-end restaurant called Summit House. It was perched atop a hill in Fullerton, and the panoramic views of North Orange County, Catalina Island, and downtown Los Angeles were spectacular. Everything was perfect. Great wine, superb food, and an amazing dessert.

It was the first meal we had eaten together in years. I can't remember what I ordered, but I know it was expensive. As my mom has always pointed out to me, I have a champagne taste on a beer budget! It's hard for me to think the Prodigal Son ate any better than I did that night.

As it turned out, that evening would prove to be the first step in restoring the broken relationship I had with my parents.

ADJUSTING TO LIFE AT HOME

After returning home, it was not as though all of my challenges cleared up overnight. I had no money and no job, and I struggled to make friends. In some respects, it was like walking back into a world where I was starting over from scratch. Those around me now had careers, spouses, and homes of their own, and I found myself connecting with those lyrics from singer Peggy Lee, "Is this all there is?"

My parents were thrilled to have me home, and I felt a freedom I had not experienced in a long time! Even though I was completely broke, I felt loved and cared for. The world might have looked at me as a failure, but I was grateful for the love and forgiveness my parents exhibited toward me. To this day, we joke about how living with my parents as a grown 28-year-old man who already had an undergraduate degree in international business and economics, a home, a business, and had traveled the world would never have been possible apart from Jesus!

Internally, I could feel a transformation taking place and noticed a period of peace, humility, thankfulness, gratefulness, and faithfulness. My parents could see this as well. Still, there was so much to work through. It was as if there was a brick wall between us, and the only way real communication could be resolved was to remove each brick, one section at a time. It was freeing and healing, and it took a lot of patience. My relationship with Dad improved, but it took years before we understood one another.

To this point, six years later and prior to marrying Amanda, I remember leading a men's group at church when a guy asked me the offhanded question of whether my dad was going to be at the bachelor party. "Not a chance," I responded. "Why would I invite him?" But the more I thought about it, I had to ask myself, *Why wouldn't I invite him?* So I did, and my dad not only came but also offered to pay for the entire event!

I share this because the healing experience I went through with my dad took many years to develop. If you are a parent in the position my dad was in at the time, don't give up! Keep tearing those bricks down one block at a time and find those points of connection—small as they might be.

> One of the greatest things my dad and I did was establish a common area of interest.

One of the greatest things my dad and I did was establish a common area of interest. We still didn't connect through activities like sports, but we found a common interest in real estate. My parents were always on the move, buying and flipping homes—riding the highs and lows of the real estate market. Their golden touch always led them to buy low and sell high. This fascinated me.

Dad and Mom had purchased some vacation properties in Big Bear, and I enjoyed helping my dad do basic home renovations such as fixing windows, installing patio decks, or painting rooms. We found common ground on topics such as politics and spent hours discussing the state of our nation.

Eventually when I entered seminary, I took my dad to class with me one day. The professor was teaching on Systematic Theology and covering topics such as God, creation, and humanity. I thought it would be a neat idea to invite my dad so he could meet some of my fellow classmates. Even though I wanted to connect with my dad on a deeper level, I held a degree of superiority and looked down on him because of his lack of spiritual knowledge.

During our class, the professor turned to my dad and posed the question, "John, what if you are the next spiritual leader of your church?" That shocked me. I couldn't believe one of my favorite seminary professors was saying something like that to my dad. Didn't she know how little he knew? But those words proved prophetic, and in the coming years, my dad would become an elder in his church.

> Returning home was not my first option, but it turned out to be God's prescription to restore the developmental void that had grown between my dad and me.

This taught me a valuable lesson. There was much he did not understand about me, but there were many things I did not value or understand about him. Together, we had much to learn.

Returning home was not my first option, but it turned out to be God's prescription to restore the developmental void that had grown between my dad and me.

STARTING TO THINK DIFFERENTLY

Outside of my family, I struggled to find meaningful relationships. In the months following my return home, I reached out to multiple local pastors in my area and asked to speak with them. I shared my journey and the struggles I faced, but not one of them followed up.

The first pastor to take an interest in my life was my high school youth intern. Steve was a bi-vocational pastor who later went full time into a family law practice. After lunch one day, he suggested we start meeting up on a regular basis. I cannot tell you what it meant to have someone who cared and acted like a friend. Our conversations began to shift the way I viewed God and the church.

Around that same time, I reached out to my childhood therapist and began sharing what God had done and how I chose to leave the gay lifestyle. As a professional, T was able to help me down an intentional path of restoration. We continued our conversation from my teenage years on what it meant to have a healthy male sexuality, and he helped me see the challenges that lay ahead. This was also healing.

My journey back to God, my family, and the church was tough but good. This time, I had nothing to hide. And despite the discomfort I felt, I sensed God was growing me up.

RETURNING TO CHURCH

I have always been an all or nothing kind of guy, so when I made the decision to come back to God, I resolved to have as much of him as I could.

Rather than being the typical churchgoer and attending one service a week, I started visiting three separate services at three different churches. Every Sunday I would attend Rose Drive Friends Church for their first morning service, then on to Yorba Linda Friends Church for the last hour of their gathering, and then I would go to Calvary Chapel Saving Grace in the evening. Never had I been hungrier for God's Word.

One might think that after coming back to faith, all of the feelings of loneliness would fade away, but that was not the case. Instead, it grew more difficult and was much different from the gay community I had left behind. They were a community with arms wide open and full of love for others. The church was not that and resorted to being a place for people who were married and had kids. If you fell outside this paradigm and into the single category, you didn't fit. I became the single male who sat alone.

Everyone else had husbands, wives, kids, or grandparents to sit beside, but each week I noticed there were at least two to three chairs in between me and anyone else around. I realized that everyone around me had other agendas on their mind and I was not one of them.

After church, I would want to meet others, shake hands, and say hello, but when people got up to leave, they turned inward—inward to themselves and those sitting next to them. I remember thinking to myself, *This is the family of God?* When I lived among those in the LGBTQ community, they embraced me with wide-open arms. But in church, I wasn't noticed and felt invisible.

> I am going to be for others what I wish someone would be for me.

There in that 1,000-seat auditorium, I began to have an internal wrestle with God in my mind. *Why me, God? You see how I am trying to serve you, yet the pain and loneliness I feel seems unbearable!*

The longer I sat there, the more I began to focus internally and think about how hard my life was. But that's when God gently whispered in my ear, "It's not about you" (Psalm 77). This got my attention, and it was as if a lightning bolt struck. My perspective shifted, and I thought to myself, *I am going to be for others what I wish someone would be for me.*

Rather than waiting for others to approach *me* and make *me* feel comfortable, I began stepping out and introducing myself to people and loving on those who sat in my area. "What's your name?" "How can I pray for you?"

It was a seismic shift from *it's all about me* to *how I can love and serve others.* That was the turning point in my life that began bringing me out of loneliness.

I remember meeting another man in church after the service. He shared a heartbreaking story with me, and I asked him if I could pray for him. It was a special moment. Right there on the spot, I placed my arm on his shoulder, we both bowed our heads, and I prayed. Immediately after the prayer, his downcast face lit up, and he smiled. I felt more blessed than him because of the joy I received from that encounter.

This might sound harsh, but I have been around enough members of the gay commu-nity to know that for the vast majority, the homosexual life is

> It was not about self; it was about sacrifice.

all about them. Just listen to the language that is often used—"It's my body." "It's my image." "It's my life." "I was born this way."

But that brings me back to Jesus, a man who was single and suffered the greatest measure of human loneliness possible. And for Him, it was not about self; it was about sacrifice. Rather than asking others to accommodate Him, He laid down His life for them.

BE THE CHANGE

I would be lying if I said I didn't go through a phase where I wanted nothing to do with church. I loved Jesus but had so many challenges with the way I saw his professing followers live their lives. All I knew was that I wanted to be Jesus with skin to a lost and dying world. I wanted to help the very person I used to be.

I remember having a conversation one night with my dad. Come to think of it, it was the first time we had a real conver-sation about sex—and I was the one who gave it! As I shared, I told him how I wanted to make a difference in the lives of others. He listened and said, "Jim, you need to have this talk with people in the church."

My internal response was, *Dad, why didn't you have this conversation with me when I was a boy?!*

Out loud, I told him I didn't think anyone would listen. He thought they would. Keep in mind this was the early 2000s. The mainstream church I knew was anti-gay and ill-equipped to deal with a community they knew nothing about.

On one hand, I wanted to attend church, but I wanted to hear little of what the church had to say on the LGB community (the days before T and Q were added). The church in America did not exactly have a good reputation with the gay community at this point, and much of that was due to misinformation and the way the church shared Jesus.

If I did choose to engage the church in this conversation, my only motivation for doing so would be because it was what God wanted me to do and it would give me an opportunity to be Jesus with skin to those who were hurting.

I contacted my two Christian friends, Chris and Michelle, and began sharing this idea and asked them to pray where it might lead.

THE FIRST TIME I SHARED MY STORY

One of the best pieces of godly counsel I received was to not share my testimony publicly until I had not acted out sexually for one year.

During that year, God began the Romans 12:1 process of transforming my life through the renewing of my mind. My ex-partner R kept calling the house and tried to lure me back, but I was in a safe, restorative respite. My folks changed their home number. The journey of healing, restoration, and spiritual wholeness I was experiencing was not one I wanted to leave.

After one year, my pastor asked me to share my story for five minutes in each of our three weekend services. Prior to sharing, a mentor of mine said it would be a good idea to tell my story to a smaller group of friends and family members first. This proved to be wise.

I shared my journey with my singles' group at church. There were about 50 people in that room, and I was amazed at the support and love I received. Many of them laid hands on me and began to pray.

Still, I was uncertain about sharing in front of our entire church. Doubt and fear began to seize me prior to the worship weekend. I was scheduled to share in a sermon series called "Will and Grace" (after the famous TV show that featured a gay lawyer and a straight interior designer) and started having second thoughts. Was I the wrong messenger?

One day as I was driving, I pulled over, opened my Bible, and turned to Isaiah 41:10 and read these comforting words:

"Fear not, for I *am* with you;
Be not dismayed, for I *am* your God.
I will strengthen you,
Yes, I will help you,
I will uphold you with My righteous right hand." (NKJV)

This was just the message I needed to hear. Several days later, I shared in front of the congregation. What happened next shocked me.

At the close of each service, dozens of people came forward to speak with me. Many of them shared how they had a loved one who was in the gay community or they were personally dealing with a similar issue. Some of them confessed to a completely different sin but felt comfortable and safe to share with me.

Through that experience, I witnessed how God was using my brokenness and same-sex attraction. He was using those years of personal failures to minister to people. Little did I know at that time just how that weekend in July of 2003 would catapult me into touching thousands of people around the globe.

I started to catch a glimpse of what might happen if I continued to share my story with more people, but it was my

> What if God could
> use my voice
> to impact those
> around the world?

mentor Steve who helped me think about it from an even broader perspective. We were sitting at a greasy diner one morning when he leaned forward, and almost in a prophetic voice he said, "Jim, instead of being a single voice, what if you were able to multiply your impact and reach more people by equipping the church? Think about this! You could increase your influence and reach more people if you trained the church with your story and could accomplish so much more than you could on your own."

That thought stuck with me. *What if God could use my voice to impact those around the world?*

WHAT HELPED ME THE MOST

Parents, it's important to note that when your child comes back to God, there will likely be a lengthy readjustment process that will almost certainly look different than you pictured in your mind.

Without stating it out loud, you, along with every other parent, have a certain set of expectations for your children. When these are not met, there is the temptation to become discouraged. For example, I struggled more than my parents would have liked to have seen. I still had many areas of selfishness that would flair up unexpectedly.

In your case, you might be praying for your child to return home when God has different ideas in mind. He might use someone else to speak into your child's life in a way that you cannot. The key here is not to grow impatient but to trust God through this journey. As you pray for Him to work in the life of your child, do not dictate your demands to Him. Let God be God.

> When your child comes back to God, there will likely be a lengthy readjustment process that will almost certainly look different than you pictured in your mind.

Keep tearing down those bricks that hold you back from having a healthy relationship. And as your child goes through this phase of readjustment, continue to meet him where he is. Adjust with him. Walk with him through the pain he is going through and be his strongest ally.

CHAPTER 9

Learning to Be Completely Alone

One of the hardest aspects of my return was the loneliness. To this day, I hate being by myself for long periods of time. I enjoy doing life with others.

The more I speak with people in the LGBTQ community, my heart continues to break as I see the pain and hurt loneliness causes in their lives. Oftentimes, it is not one major event but the sequence of isolating events that cause many to shrivel up on the inside and die a slow death.

My personal feelings of loneliness started the moment I realized I had feelings for boys my age, and that is not normal. There was this secret part of my life that no one else could enter, and that in itself was isolating. Compound this with when I hit high school and my younger brother by two years started to take girls out on dates and my younger sister by seven years showed an equal interest in boys.

And then there was me, Jim, the first-born child, with little hope or desire for prospects of the opposite sex. Sure, I tried the dating game and even had a girlfriend for a short stint in college, but this relationship quickly fizzled.

I say this not to gain sympathy but to give you an inside perspective of how lonely it can feel to live with same-sex attraction in a world that prioritizes opposite sex relationships.

THE DREADED HOLIDAYS

Holidays were the worst. My brother Jeff got married in 1998, and this only added to the comments that came my way. Questions like "Jim, when is it your turn?" were sometimes too much to take. Thanksgiving, Christmas, and New Year's Eve were times of joy for others but seasons of dread for me.

November and December remain some of the toughest months for members of the gay community. Thanksgiving, as I was taught, was a time family and loved ones came together to celebrate their gratefulness, thankfulness, and blessings. Yet for me, it was a constant reminder of what I would not be able to have—a girlfriend or wife.

Christmas was even more heartbreaking. Despite it being my favorite holiday for decades, the thought of never having children who would experience the joys of Christmas Eve, Christmas morning, and Christmas dinner was overwhelming and continued to reveal what I didn't have and would not be able to experience as a gay man.

Even though the nieces and nephews loved me and called me their favorite "Crazy Uncle Jim," the smile on my face was all I could muster to cover the true pain I felt inside. All of the time spent buying clothes for my nieces and nephews, coloring giant words and pictures on cards filled with cash, or buying live animals from pet stores was fulfilling in the moment but did little to ease my pain as I went to sleep that night.

New Year's Day kicked off each year with another reminder that I was not normal. After all, who do you kiss at midnight when you are attracted to the same sex and everyone else is kissing their significant other of the opposite sex?

Then there's Valentine's Day, the worst holiday of all. I hated it. It seemed to me the entire world was against me on this day, doing its best to make it as miserable as possible. I would often think to myself, *Just rub it in, everybody—you with your holiday created for florists, candy makers, and card designers to bolster the discontentment of those not having a significant other of the opposite sex!*

It's for this reason those in the LGBTQ community have come up with their own parties. When I lived in Palm Springs, I remember taking part in the annual White Party at Easter—a celebration geared toward gay men. In case you are unfamiliar, White Party was a weeklong event with half-clothed or naked men who drank, danced, and did whatever was pleasurable in the moment. I remember the first time I attended one of these celebrations. I couldn't help but think to myself, *Now this is a holiday I can enjoy!* A few months after White Party is Gay Pride Day followed by Halloween (a major holiday for members of the LGBTQ community) in the fall.

Traditional holidays are some of the most miserable times of the year for people attracted to the same sex, not just because of the loneliness but also the rejection. Again, not to get ahead of the story, but when I came out as gay, I remember more than one friend having an awkward conversation with me, telling me I was no longer welcome in their home.

Embedded in my mind was an awkward conversation that took place after my brother's wedding in June of 1998. I had made plans to stay with a friend from college and her family in Dallas. She was married and had a young son. As I traveled from Austin to Dallas to stay the night prior to my plane's departure, I received a call that nearly crushed me. She said, "Uh, Jim, I had a talk with my husband, and I'm sorry, but you will not be able to stay with us." Apparently, the news that I was gay had gotten around.

This was supposed to be a Christian family, but in one conversation I felt our relationship had been cut for good. *Is this the way Christians treat people?* I thought.

In that moment, my emotional ache was so great that I purchased a hotel room and acted out sexually with a man that night. It was all I could do to keep from feeling miserable. Like the holidays, it was a reminder that I lived in a world of isolation.

DYING ALONE

All of this brings to mind a recent letter I received from a pastor's wife after Christmas a short time ago. Her son "J" deals with same-sex attraction, and through the 2020 holiday season (in the midst of the Covid pandemic), they had an honest conversation that brought tears to my eyes.

After a few introductory remarks, she shared this story:

J was tearful for part of Christmas day. We could see the battle inside him to engage and participate in the games with his siblings or isolate himself and check out. I spoke with him this morning about those emotions. The conversation started because we got him a music production class as a gift. We were hoping to give him some motivation as he has been very lost since leaving his school in Hollywood.

We thought it might spark some creativity and engage hope, but it didn't. It sparked tears and the reverse emotions. I was trying to understand how he was feeling and asked if he wanted us to return the gift and just give him money. He said he doesn't think he can write songs anymore and has no desire to live, and if God doesn't do something soon, he will take his life.

Those words were jarring. He stated that he feels like though he is only twenty, his time is running out and that God took school away to punish him.

I asked, "Punish you for what, son? For feeling gay?" He nodded. He said he sat with his siblings on Christmas, watching them share gifts with their spouses, fiancé, and children and that he will never have that. He felt his only choice was to be celibate and pursue acting and performing and stay busy 100% of the time to fill the void and that he'd never truly belong or fit in.

He says he can't marry a girl and lie to her and ruin her life and any children's lives and could never bring a guy home. He's angry at God for yanking school and performing away with Covid and that a God who loves him would have taken this feeling away after years of praying and pleading. He feels like God took school away to punish him and now he won't have performing to occupy his mind so all he can think about is what a failure and screw up he is and can't figure out what he did to mess himself up so badly.

He says he loves God in spite of being angry, even though his friends who spit in God's face are living happily and getting engaged.

The experience J expressed is one that plays itself out not just on holidays but any occasion when the "norm of life" is celebrated.

A VOICE FOR THE VOICELESS

Through my extended periods of personal loneliness, I have discovered that God has increased my compassion for those who suffer in silence. In a sense, He has given me a voice for the voiceless.

Perhaps one of the reasons this concept resonates with me so much goes back to a point in my life when I literally lost my voice for several months. From 1998 to 2002, I had smoked a pack of cigarettes every day. Follow this with my time as a pastor and a natural talker, and my vocal cords took a big hit. By 2011 while I was on staff at a church, I had developed a nodule (a growth of abnormal tissue or perhaps better described as a cyst) on one of my vocal cords.

> Through my extended periods of personal loneliness, I have discovered that God has increased my compassion for those who suffer in silence.

After receiving a professional opinion from one of the best vocal experts in southern California, I had the cyst removed and biopsied. Thankfully, it was benign, but this procedure meant I was unable to talk for six weeks. It was my doctor's opinion that vocal rest was what I needed most and that this would bring about the strongest recovery.

While the cyst removal gave me my voice back, I discovered there was a new battle I faced the moment I went back to work. Everyone treated me differently.

"HOW ARE YOU DOING, JIM?! ARE YOU FEELING OK?!" someone would shout at me as though my inability to speak affected my ability to hear.

I promise it took everything in me not to sarcastically write back on a dry-erase board in bold letters, "MY HEARING AND BRAIN ARE FINE. I JUST CAN'T SPEAK!"

As this happened, I realized how those around me did not know how to respond. For the next few weeks, it was if I had been written off as an afterthought. We would hold staff meetings, but because I could not speak, my opinion no longer seemed to matter, and others talked as though I did not exist.

Because I am an extrovert who processes my thoughts out loud, the experience was especially isolating, and those six weeks felt like an eternity. But here is what I discovered. Because I could no longer speak, I was forced into silence, and that resulted in better discerning the voice of God. As my world ground to a halt, God was on the move, and as it turned out, it was in the midst of that season when the seeds for my organization, Church United, were sown. Today, I can say that period of my life was one of the greatest blessings I have ever received—not because I enjoyed the experience, but because it heightened my dependency on God and increased my empathy for others.

AN ENCOURAGEMENT TO YOUR CHILD

Parents, be sensitive to the loneliness your gay son might feel. Remember that when he comes back to God, this is where an even greater battle begins. Now is not the time to breathe a sigh of relief, thank God he is back, and pause your prayers. Rather, it's critical you continue to pray for him and intercede on his behalf.

> It was his patience and encouragement that shifted me from focusing on myself to being a source of hope to others.

Do whatever you can to make those lonely moments less painful. Be open with your child. Talk to him. Ask him how he is feeling and for ways you can love him better. Communicate that you care.

It was my dad who planted seeds for me to share my story with others. It was his patience and encouragement that shifted me from focusing on myself to being a source of hope to others.

You can do this with your child.

CHAPTER 10

Healthy Male Sexuality

What does it mean to be a man? This was a question I often asked myself after I came back to God. There are so many thoughts that come to mind.

As I think through this chapter, I am sitting next to my free-standing gun safe that contains my 300 Winchester Mangum rifle, AR 15, shotgun, 22 rifle, and an entire arsenal of ammunition. I've got six months of growth on my beard and mustache, and by many people's standards, I look like a "man's man."

Even my barber made this remark the other day, "Jim, real men have guns, beards, and drive a truck." This made me laugh because I checked the first two boxes but not the third. Apparently, my manhood is continuing to mature!

The topic of manhood takes me back to my interesting heritage. My dad is of Eastern European descent while my mom is from Western Europe. Both are ethnic mutts with a variety of backgrounds making up their family tree. In Europe, the idea of being a man is different from the States. True men do not necessarily wear a cowboy hat and ride a horse, though I've done this too! They come in all different forms. There are men who exhibit what the typical American might see as effeminate qualities, but to those in their culture they are "masculine."

I think for most Americans, when they think of the term "manly," they think of the Discovery Channel's Bear Grylls flying to remote places to survive the wilderness by eating insects and escaping nature's harshest elements. Whenever I think of the term, my first image is of a warrior. I picture a Navy Seal as someone who embodies all that it means to be a man.

But the problem is that everyone's idea of manhood looks different in each context. It is subjective. For Jewish people, there is the Bar Mitzvah that celebrates a Jewish youth's coming of age. For other tribal societies, this step into manhood is consummated with a hunt in the wild. To many in America, manhood is that point when you take your first drink of alcohol. Almost every culture has some life event where men affirm their son's transition from boy to man.

THE FOUR MODELS OF MANHOOD

My counselor T was the one who helped me understand what true masculinity was all about. He introduced me to the author Robert Bly, a man who was part of the secular men's movement in the 80s and 90s. I read his book, *Iron John,* and connected with his in-depth look at the German folklore story of a boy who was led into manhood by a wild man.

Another book that changed my thinking was Robert Moore's book, *King, Warrior, Magician, Lover: Rediscovering the Archetypes of the Mature Masculine.* In it, Moore took these four words and gave me a better understanding of what true masculinity was all about.

The *Warrior* is the fighter who stands for what is right. It's the Navy Seal who liberates those enslaved by sex trafficking and drug lords. It's the husband who will protect his wife at all costs and stands against injustice. And it's the average citizen that pushes back against government oppression and fights against corrupt politicians. Being a warrior does not always mean pulling out a sword. It means fighting for what is right.

Next is the *Magician*. The magician is the initiation, transformation, and healing parts of the masculine soul. I equate it to man's drive to fix or correct what is not right and place things in order.

The *Lover* is an expression of sexuality but is not just about sex. It's how you win a woman's heart and involves wooing your wife with daily romance to win her affection. This also includes loving your daughters just like a man should. This is demonstrated by showing them how a man honors and protects them—from opening doors and treating them with kindness and snuggling with them at night—to shielding from harm.

And finally, there is the *King*. Not someone who rules over their household with an iron fist, but a man who takes on the role as the leader of his home. It's leading by example and being a provider for the home. You are setting a positive example for your family to walk in your steps.

These four descriptions changed my thought process on what it meant to be a man, and I started trying to incorporate them into my daily behavior.

OBEDIENCE TO GOD'S WORD

As Christopher Yuan writes, "Holy sexuality is not focused on orientation change—becoming straight—but on obedience. And I realized that obedience means, no matter what my situation, no matter what my feelings—gay or straight—I must obey and be faithful to God."[16]

For me, obedience meant understanding what the Bible said on the topic of homosexuality and submitting my desires to God's instruction. I refocused my attention on some of the key passages in Scripture that addressed this issue (six in total) but also looked at the broader meta narrative of the Bible.

I saw that the Bible wasn't all about having a few bully verses that were intended to discriminate against those in the LGBTQ community. Instead, I saw a story God was painting throughout human history—a story that included my life.

> Obey God first, and trust Him for the grace and freedom He will provide.

Some inside the church might wonder why I cannot affirm same-sex relationships or same-sex marriages that are between two committed individuals. After all, isn't the Bible all about love? And what could be more loving than two people who are committed to one another? But again, when I look at Scripture, I see no evidence the Bible affirms same-sex relationships.

Again, I have seen many pastors and parents with sympathetic hearts try to do some form of intellectual gymnastics to suggest the Bible is indeed affirming of gay relationships, but I personally see little compelling evidence for how this can be the case. In the end, more harm than good comes from that approach.

This brings me back to the topic of obedience. The longer I've walked with God and lived as He has called me to live, the greater the freedom I have experienced. I love these words from former lesbian Rosaria Butterfield, "When Christ gave me the strength to follow him, I didn't stop feeling like a lesbian. I've discovered that the Lord doesn't change my feelings until I obey him."[17] That has been my story.

Obey God first, and trust Him for the grace and freedom He will provide.

INSTILLING SEXUALITY PRINCIPLES IN MY KIDS

Now that I am a dad, I think of healthy male sexuality not only for myself but also for my son. It's not just about making sure I am making the right choices, but it is about fostering an environment where my son can become the man God intends him to be.

To do this, I must get on his level. When our son was born, I remember holding him tight to my chest and doing that skin-to-skin connection our nurse said was important. As he and my two girls entered their developmental years, Amanda and I taught them what their body parts were and not to be ashamed of them. My boy knew he had a penis, and my girls knew they had vaginas. These weren't awkward conversations because we had them early and often.

As my son has grown, I have taught him to enjoy masculine things. We shoot guns, and he takes his little Red Daisy BB gun. Amanda does a great job with our girls and models what it means to be feminine in dress and behavior.

It's not as though we have this lengthy set of exclusive activities where only boys shoot guns while the girls play with their hair and makeup. Sometimes Amanda does my son's hair, and sometimes my girls go shooting. But in these activities, we are being intentional in how we guide their interactions.

It all comes back to getting on their level. Whenever my dad corrected me, he was always higher and pointing his finger. It was sort of the king and a pauper scene. He was up there; I was down here. Subtly, this created a gap in our relationship, and I viewed him as unapproachable.

Now, whenever I connect with my kids (especially if I am upset), I get down on their level. I kneel in front of them, get eye to eye, and have a conversation. If they have just come out of timeout, I ask, "Why were you in a timeout?"

Sometimes they respond with, "I don't know." And then I explain. "Son, the reason you were in timeout is because you pushed your sister and she scraped her knee."

> Sometimes my kids are the teacher while I am the student.

Usually, they will apologize to me, but I ask them to take their apology a step further. I ask them to go find their sibling and ask for their forgiveness. Then, I always instruct them to ask this question, "What can I do to make it better?" The response is often something simple like "I just want a hug" or "Could you kiss my knee?"

The whole point of this little exercise is face-to-face communication. I am getting on their level and teaching them how to interact in healthy and loving ways.

It is only fair to point out that sometimes my kids are the teacher while I am the student. Not long ago, I was having a frustrating day and made a series of sharp statements. That's when my older girl, who was seven at the time, said, "You know, Daddy, the words you are using aren't very kind."

I knew she was right, and it took me straight to my knees. I looked at my daughter and asked her to forgive me. She looked at me with those big hazel eyes, as little girls do, and said, "Yes, Daddy, I forgive you."

Then there was the other day when my son started sniffling and said to me, "Daddy, you hurt my feelings." He was right.

"Son, Daddy is in a bad mood, but can you forgive Daddy? I was wrong."

To see this little guy's face turn from tears to a big smile was beautiful. It reminds me that whenever I mess up, I can make it right. In doing so, I become a role model for my kids and teach them how to handle their own mistakes.

KEEP TRYING

Part of being a good parent is admitting when you're wrong. As you have gone through this book, it's possible you have experienced some feelings of guilt about the way you raised your children. You look at my story and can't help comparing it to your child. I get it.

But if you are a dad, my encouragement to you is to find ways to model to your son what it means to be a healthy man. He might not be at an age where you have to bend down to look him in the eye, but you can still get on his level.

Dads, if your son is still at home, model for him what healthy male sexuality looks like. Moms, if your teenage son is still clinging to your apron strings, talk to your husband and make sure he is engaged. Single moms, find some good men in your church who would be willing to let your son hang out with their families from time to time so they can see how healthy males interact. Sometimes, it's the seemingly small steps that have a significant impact.

A number of years ago, I was working with a high school group at our church when a single mom approached me and asked for help. "Would you mind spending some time with my twin boys?" she asked. "They keep getting into trouble at school and home. I am not sure what to do with them and the principal recommended I reach out to male role models."

I wasn't sure what to tell her, but I said we could meet. It was awkward because I quickly found out we had almost nothing in common! All these boys cared about was video games, and I hadn't played one in years.

But over the next year, we started spending more time together. If we were at church together, I made it a point to interact with them. Before long, we developed a friendship.

Years later, Amanda and I had them over for dinner. They were in college by this point. From my vantage point, the investment I had made in their lives was minimal. But as they shared that evening, those interactions I had with them were pivotal in their development. My voice in their life played a small role in helping them become the healthy men they are today.

> I had shifted from being the guy who *needed* help to *being a help* to others.

Doing some reflection on this conversation, I couldn't help but think how my life had started to come full circle. I had shifted from being the guy who *needed* help to *being a help* to others.

It showed me that change was possible.

CHAPTER 11

Change Is Possible

It's not as if you can take a red or blue pill that will switch your desires from homosexual to heterosexual overnight. But I have found you can take specific actions that are more masculine and in alignment with God's intended design for your life. It's even better if you surround yourself with people who will speak life into you.

My wife has been one of those people. On our honeymoon in Rome, my wife observed the many naked male statues and told me, "You know, Jim, your body is even better looking than these statues." Her simple comment meant so much because I had always thought poorly of my body, and I just assumed I would never measure up. But Amanda taught me that healthy words can correct unhealthy thoughts and perspectives.

> Healthy words can correct unhealthy thoughts and perspectives.

The more I focused on doing masculine things and responding in masculine ways, my involuntary responses began to change.

Again, it was Amanda who pointed this out to me. We were lying in bed one night, and sometime around 2 a.m., we heard this tremendous crash. Instantly, I jumped out of bed and bolted toward the commotion. It could have been an earthquake or a burglar for all I knew, but I was on the move! After a bit of investigating, I discovered it was just the dog knocking something off the counter. Returning to bed, I found my wife hiding under the covers with her eyes peeking out from the sheets.

> Make conscious decisions to choose masculinity as I have done.

As she pointed out, our responses couldn't have been more different. She exhibited the need for protection, and I stepped in as the protector. Years before, I am confident I would not have made the same decision. I would have probably remained with my wife under the covers till morning!

I make this point to emphasize that change is possible. It isn't easy, but you can be mentored and make conscious decisions to choose masculinity as I have done. As Sam Allberry points out, "It is not un-Christian to experience same-sex attraction any more than it is un-Christian to get sick. What marks us out as Christian is not that we never experience such things, but how we respond to them when we do."[18]

THE GOAL IS NOT GAY TO STRAIGHT

Ultimately, changing someone from gay to straight is not the goal. That is not what the Christian message is all about. It all comes back to identity. Our primary identity is in Christ, and He becomes the source of all our happiness. Sin needs to be addressed, but that is part of the journey with Jesus.

Several years ago, a pastor reached out because a man came to the front of the church after a Sunday service and sensed God was speaking to him about his same-sex activity. My pastor gave this man my number, and he gave me a call. The first words out of his mouth went something like this, "Listen, I know you're a pastor that has come out of the homosexual lifestyle, but I hope you're not trying to get me to go from gay to straight!"

I started laughing. "Look, buddy, that's not my goal," I reassured him. "Tell me what Jesus is doing in your life. Why did you come forward, and what is God speaking to you?" That simple response defused the tension, and this man went on to share how God was convicting him of acting out sexually with other men.

Notice the difference in this approach. I could have said, "Hi there, I'm Jim! I used to be in the gay lifestyle, but now I am married and have a wonderful wife and kids. If you get right with Jesus, you can have this too!"

If I had used that approach, I would have been using Jesus as a means to an end. But what I try to help people like this man understand is that Jesus *is* the end. In Him, we can discover satisfaction.

SOMETIMES PEOPLE DO NOT REALIZE WHAT THEY SAY

While I was on staff as a pastor at a church, I had a woman approach me with a piece of paper. She handed it to me, and I could see it had a Scripture reference I did not recognize. Looking into my eyes, she whispered those words I have come to view with a degree of apprehension, "God told me to share this with you."

She had my attention. The passage was Matthew 19:12 which says, "For there are eunuchs who were born that way, and there are eunuchs who have been made eunuchs by others—and there are those who choose to live like eunuchs for the sake of the kingdom of heaven. The one who can accept this should accept it."

Her point was clear. I was to remain single all of my life and accept this as my cross to bear. As I look back on this brief encounter, it was one of the most hurtful conversations I ever experienced. This lady knew little about me, and I can look back and say her message was certainly not from God. And despite any well-meaning intentions she had, the pain she caused was much greater than any comfort she intended.

Contrast this story with the same-sex-attracted pastor, Sam Allberry. Sam loves Jesus but believes the life he is called to presently live is one of celibacy. But like myself, he too experienced a painful encounter which he shares in his book, *Is God Anti-Gay?* He writes, "I remember meeting another pastor who, on finding out I was single, was insistent that I should be married by now and proceeded to outline immediate steps I needed to take to rectify this. He was very forthright and only backed down when I burst into tears and told him I was struggling with homosexuality. It is not an admission I should have needed to make. We need to respect that singleness is not necessarily a sign that someone is postponing growing up."[19]

More than once, I have heard a well-meaning Christian speak of the gay community and say something like, "Well, you just need to love the sinner but hate the sin!" But it's just these kinds of unbiblical trite phrases that can bring an extraordinary amount of pain to those who are on the receiving end. To the LGBTQ people who believe their sexual orientation is their identity, all they hear this person say is that they hate gay people. This only pushes them farther away.

When you have a conversation with a gay person, your goal is not to offer platitudes or make up some prophetic word for their life. Your goal is to point him to the ultimate truth, Jesus Christ. He is the only truth that sets people free.

SOMETIMES THE CHAINS OF OUR PAST RESURFACE

While the freedom Christ offers is sufficient to confront every temptation we face, the chains of our past sometimes resurface. Like voices in the darkness, they call out to us, inviting us to go back to the life we have left behind.

Writing this next section pains me more than I care to admit. After my return to Christ in 2002, there was one key relapse that almost took me back into the world I thought I left behind.

The year was 2005, and I was in seminary. That was when I met a fellow student. At the time, he was married and serving as a pastor. "V" was tall, dark, handsome, and winsome. He was a muscular 6'1" jock, and we had an instant attraction. We became good friends and worked out together.

The very first time we hung out together, I vividly recall God saying, "Do not move forward with this friendship." I thought to myself, *God, come on! V is a pastor. He's a great guy, and we have so many similar interests. We connect spiritually, socially, and emotionally. We understand each other even though we come from different pasts of sin issues. Besides, he doesn't even deal with same-sex attraction!*

My refusal to listen to God's voice gave birth to a secret, lust-filled relationship. I was on a pastoral staff and looked forward to those times I could be with V. We carpooled together, worked out together, and studied for finals together. His wife knew we were spending a lot of time together, but she never suspected it was an unhealthy relationship.

The longer the relationship lasted, the more we opened up with one another. We shared struggles and failures, and he told me about the marital issues he was having. We talked a lot about the flesh and the sexual desires of the flesh. Each time we spent time together and talked about sexual things, I was always aroused.

Once again, God intervened in my life and spoke through my two friends, Steve and Richard. Both of them warned me that this friendship was heading down a wrong path, and if I was not careful, I would fall into sexual sin.

I did not want to hear it. On one hand, I heard what they were saying, but in the back of my mind, I kept saying I was strong enough to ward off any temptations I faced.

Then things took a turn for the worse. I was still living with my parents while attending seminary. One night, V and I were studying late for finals in my parents' two-story, 3,500-square-foot home. I had my own room and private bathroom downstairs that resembled a granny suite or butler's quarters. I told my parents we were studying late and asked if V could spend the night in one of the rooms upstairs. They agreed, and Mom got one of their extra guest bedrooms ready.

We were studying in my room with the door closed and V suddenly grew "tired." He laid on his back with his hands interlocked behind his head. Even though he closed his eyes, I knew he wasn't asleep. Looking back, I knew he was testing the waters to see if I would take the bait and commit some sexual act.

Somewhat miraculously, I did not.

V "woke up" shortly afterwards and turned in for the night in the upstairs bedroom, but he wasn't done trying. The next morning, he called down and said he needed a towel. My parents were out, so we were all alone once again. Walking up the stairs, I could hear the water running in the shower. He opened the door a crack and gave me a Cheshire cat smile, tempting me to come in and pleasure him and myself.

But once again, I resisted. I handed him the towel and walked downstairs. As I look back on that day, I am grateful for God's strength, but I am likewise ashamed of my disobedience. I knew he had warned me. I knew he had used others to warn me. And still I ignored him.

Following our school finals week, I decided to heed the counsel of my friends and end my relationship with V. I'll never forget that day. We had just finished working out at a 24-Hour Fitness in Anaheim Hills. Our tradition was to grab a protein smoothie across the street while we cooled down and talked some more about life. But this day was different. I told V that I had to end our friendship.

In that moment, I never recalled seeing a man get as angry as he did. With angry darts shooting from his eyes, he stood up and pushed the table at me. As he stormed off, he picked up a chair and threw it across the shop. I followed him out to the parking lot to help him process his thoughts.

It was then he shared something that shocked me, "Jim, I'm really impressed. You surprised me. You did not give in. I've never had a man not give in or want to have sex with me."

Dumbfounded, I walked away and never spoke with V again. It was a Thursday, and because I had Friday off, I took a drive to the mountains to visit Big Bear Lake. I will never forget that drive. It was a beautiful day and turned out to be one of the greatest times I have ever spent with God. But as I drove, something happened that I had never experienced before. It was as if something broke inside me, and I wept as I had never wept before.

I cried so hard, it was a miracle the car remained on the road. In that 90-minute drive, the grace of God flooded into my soul, and I knew God cared. I repeated the song "Only You" by David Crowder during that drive, and the lyrics represented my repentant heart of worshipping something created instead of the Creator.

Apart from the grace of God, I should have fallen. Only God.

SEEING MY SAME-SEX ATTRACTION AS AN OPPORTUNITY

Ever since the seventh grade, I spent hours pleading with God to take away my same-sex desires. In 2007, I took a tour to Israel with my seminary.

Initially, I didn't want to go. I was a pastor at the time and didn't feel like spending $4,000 to spend two weeks doing more "Christian work." But after my grandma, parents, and the university chipped in $1,000 a piece, I had no excuse to say no, so I grudgingly laid aside my plans to vacation two weeks on the beach and boarded a plane to the Middle East.

> Why won't you take this attraction away God? I have asked you for years, and it feels like all I hear is silence. Why won't you answer me? Why don't you fix me?

That trip changed my life.

Day after day the Bible kept coming more alive, giving me fresh perspective. It was a surreal experience to walk through the same territory Jesus traveled and shifted the way I viewed Scripture. Our tour guide was amazing and did all he could to help us see life through the eyes of those who lived 2000 years before.

One stop took us to the shores of the Zarqa River, known in the Old Testament as Jabbok. This marked the spot where Jacob wrestled an angel. I thought of my own wrestling match with God and kind of envied Jacob. His match only lasted a night, whereas mine lasted 21 years.

Near the end of our tour, our group stopped at the Garden of Gethsemane. As I walked through this sacred space and pictured what Jesus must have thought about on that night before His death, my mind drifted to my own struggle. I found a spot alone by myself and cracked open my Bible to spend some time in silent meditation.

That was when all of the thoughts I struggled with for years came to the forefront of my mind. I remembered thinking,

> My grace is sufficient for you, for my power is made perfect in weakness.

Why won't you take this attraction away, God? I have asked you for years, and it feels like all I hear is silence. Why won't you answer me? Why don't you fix me? It was one of the reasons why I went to seminary. I wanted to be healed and fixed.

As my attention turned to Matthew 26, I thought of the three times Jesus asked God to take away the bitter cup He was about to drink. But at the end of these pleas, He finished with these words, "Yet not as I will, but as you will."

It seemed as if God was saying to me in this moment, "You see, Jim, even Jesus pled three times, and the response was silence in Scripture's account."

My first response was, "Yeah, God, but Jesus only pled three times. I've been pleading for years!"

But then I sensed God direct my attention to another man in the New Testament who pleaded three times—the Apostle Paul. In 2 Corinthians 12:8-9, after pleading with God three times to take away his thorn in the flesh, Paul received this response, "My grace is sufficient for you, for my power is made perfect in weakness."

Perfect in weakness. Those words resonated with my spirit because I felt so weak and incapable of continuing on the way I had been. But in that moment, the cloud of "wanting to get fixed" lifted. And from that moment on, I stopped trying to pray the gay away because it was through this struggle that I realized my deep need for God.

I experienced unmistakable hope.

Part 3

Unmistakable Hope

CHAPTER 12

A Divine Mistake

I began dating girls in 2005. During that season, I was a full-time singles' pastor at my church. When word got out that I was interested in having a girlfriend, every match maker in the country seemed to offer their expert advice.

But at age 31, my options were limited. The running joke among Christian singles my age was that there was a reason someone was in their early 30s and still not taken.

My early days of dating did little to dispel this myth. I dated every type of girl you might imagine. I went out with the tall, short, godly, and ungodly as well as girls who were nice, but we never seemed to click. Never once did I sense peace. There was always some sort of problem in the way. I was too liberal or too conservative for their liking. They were too serious or not serious enough for mine. All of those relationships started to confirm in my mind the notion that I really was a mistake.

> Now that I was attracted to members of the opposite sex and wanted a healthy relationship, it seemed wrong that not one relationship would work out.

By 2008, I'd had enough. I remember telling God I was through dating and was going to instead focus on his kingdom. For years, my only desire had been same-sex relationships. Now that I was attracted to members of the opposite sex and wanted a healthy relationship, it seemed wrong that not one relationship would work out.

"All of the good girls are already taken," I told God. "And what's more, I'm good with that!"

But God had other plans.

MEETING AMANDA

My dating life was fun and my relationship with God was at an all-time high. There was this passion that I had to share Jesus with others, and this compelled me to learn more about my faith. From 2002 to 2006, I was in school at Azusa Pacific University, attempting to earn a Master of Divinity, even becoming the Senior Speaker of my graduating class. When I went to Israel in 2007, all I had left to complete was my thesis. It was like that pesky rock in my shoe that wouldn't go away. Every time I thought about working on it, some distraction would get in the way.

But on that trip, one of my college professors challenged me to set aside time and finish what I had started. After this conversation, I resolved to do as he challenged. My area of focus was on the topic of discipleship, and that next year I successfully defended my thesis in front of three of my college professors.

Because I had already walked and spoken for my class, all the school needed was my final grade so they could post my degree and release my diploma. That was fine with me. The only problem was they mailed my diploma to the wrong address. Several weeks later, I received a call saying it was at the graduate center and I could pick it up any time.

I knew how much effort this degree took and wasn't about to let this little inconvenience get in the way. That afternoon, I drove over to the school on my lunch break, slightly annoyed.

As I walked into the graduate center, I was distracted and talking to someone on my cell phone. When I got up to the counter, I hit mute and asked the front desk worker for my diploma. The girl standing there told me I would need my ID, and this only heightened my annoyance. Rolling my eyes, I ran back to my car, finished my call, and came back to give her my card. When I did, she looked through her files and handed me a large manilla envelope.

"Why don't you open it?" she suggested. "You worked very hard for your degree, and you should take it out and look at your diploma."

Determined as I was to beat the rush-hour traffic on my return to the office, I pulled it out, started reading, and almost came to tears. As I thought back on all I experienced over the last several years, the moment felt especially emotional.

"This is a miracle," I mumbled aloud. "I cannot believe what God has done. I have come out of the homosexual lifestyle. I've just bought my first home. I'm a pastor, and now I have a Master of Divinity." As soon as I said this, the girl behind the desk responded with a statement that shocked me.

"It sounds as if God has restored the years the locusts have eaten."

I froze. *Who is this girl that knows Joel 2?* I said to myself. Most Christians I interacted with did not know their Bible like that. And it wasn't just what she said but how she said it. I could tell something was different about her, and I could see Jesus in her eyes.

She went on to share that she had friends in the gay community. This also got my attention. My statement that I had left the homosexual lifestyle was not a red flag to her. She understood.

After some small chitchat, I got her number. But being a little timid, I didn't come right out and ask for it. I found out she was a semi-professional oboe player and told her I should definitely get her number since my church hired an orchestra at Christmas time.

She consented, and I also discovered her name—Amanda.

After saying goodbye, I headed back to my church office, feeling somewhat guilty as I drove. *Why was I so scared? Why didn't I ask her out that first time we met?* After calling one of my friends, I resolved to man up and conquer my fears. Because I got her cell number sneakily, I knew the right thing to do was to call her office. The next day, I did just that. Her assistant answered the phone and said Amanda was in a meeting.

It's over, I thought to myself. *She has pulled the old "I'm in a meeting" card so she will never have to talk to me*! But to my surprise, she called back later that afternoon. Her voice sounded angelic. After some first-time small talk, I asked if she was married. She said she wasn't, and I invited her out for coffee.

October 13, 2008, was the start of something special.

THIS GIRL IS DIFFERENT

The next day, Amanda and I met at a Starbucks just down the street from where she worked. It was clear from our conversation that she was different from any other girl I had dated before. I discovered she was 30 years of age and the associate director in one of the graduate offices. Normally, she didn't even work at the front desk, so the fact we met was what you might call a divine mistake.

It was obvious she had a missional heart and deep love for those in need. On Friday nights she played oboe with a church group for a service at The Salvation Army's free drug and alcohol rehabilitation program. On top of her generous heart to play for free, she also taught a weekly women's Bible study and had done so for 14 years before we met.

The stories she shared both saddened and amused me. I'll never forget some of the questions she was asked by women in her group who knew nothing of God. Questions like, "Was Mary really a virgin? Are you sure she didn't just get really drunk one night and forget what happened?" "If Jesus is his first name, is Christ his last name?" She had heard it all. What I loved about Amanda was her Christlike heart and patience to walk with women through their pain and little knowledge about God.

The more we talked, the more I sensed God say *this* was the girl I was going to marry. Of course, I wasn't about to tell her that and kept this secret between me and God.

One of the things about Amanda I appreciated was the way she treated me. She knew her boundaries, was confident in herself, and did not need me to complete her life's dreams. This became evident when I leaned forward for that all important first kiss—my way of saying she was special. Every other girl I dated before had no problem with this. Amanda was different.

"I don't kiss guys unless I'm in a committed relationship, and right now, I am seeing other guys," she said.

This pushback against my "irresistible charm" surprised me, but I laughed internally because I knew what she was doing. She was taking the game I always played with girls and throwing it right back in my face! It was her way of saying, "Not so fast, cowboy! You seem like a great guy, but you are far from the only male in this universe!" That was just what I needed. Before Amanda, I was used to telling girls things like, "Just because I kiss you, it doesn't mean I am going to marry you." It was my game. My rules. But this girl was different.

So, I licked my wounds of pride, settled for a hug goodbye, and counted it a massive victory when she agreed to go out with me again.

GOD WAS WORKING IN AMANDA'S HEART

Even though Amanda put on a strong front, I knew God was working in her life, just as He had been in mine.

Later in our relationship, I learned some of the behind-the-scenes details. As it turned out, my call to ask her for a date was not a complete surprise. In fact, she had been expecting it. As soon as I walked out of her office that day, several of her co-workers started teasing her about the connection we made. Even at that early stage, others could see we were a good fit.

Here is Amanda's perspective of the day we met and our first date:

Jim and I met on Monday, October 13th, 2008. It was a mistake that turned out to be the best thing ever for me. I was 30 years old, and I wanted to be married, but I hadn't dated any guys I could see myself marrying. I had taken dating so seriously in the past that it put pressure on myself (and the men I dated) to decide about marriage, and it wasn't a healthy mindset for me.

I had recently read the book, How to Get a Date Worth Keeping by Cloud and Townsend and was applying their advice to lighten things up and go out with anyone once, maybe twice. It was much healthier for me to broaden my scope of dating to relax and take time to get to know someone.

I was not relaxing my standards, just taking the pressure off. I had been telling all the guys I went out with that I was open to meeting guys and dating, but I wasn't looking to be exclusive with any one guy, at least at this time.

It was a regular Monday, and I was working as a supervisor in one of the graduate offices at Azusa Pacific University. I was not usually behind the front desk because my office was in the back, but I was checking in with my team and happened to be sitting right at the reception desk, when in walked Jim Domen. Our office had mailed his diploma, but it returned with an undeliverable address, so Jim needed to come in person to pick it up.

Jim walked into the office, and at first, he seemed too busy to talk. When I handed him his diploma, I could see the emotion on his face, and Jim started sharing about what Jesus had done in his life. He never thought he would get a seminary degree because God had brought him out of the gay lifestyle, and now he had been a pastor for five years at a great church. God had given him so much because he had just bought his first house, too.

I said, "It sounds like God has restored the years the locusts have eaten!" I was blown away by this man who had just walked into our office checking off the boxes of what I was looking for! On fire for Jesus Christ (check one), has a good job (check two), has a house (check three), and he's good looking (check four)! I needed to get to know this man.

He did ask for my phone number, but it was to connect me with the music director at his church to audition to play oboe with their orchestra. After Jim left the office, several ladies in my office teased me about the connection we had just made. I knew that Jim would be calling me, and I knew I wanted to get to know him better. But what about the part where he used to be gay? It didn't scare me because I knew God could change a person, though perhaps a part of me was hesitant.

That evening I spoke to my mom—a wonderful godly woman and prayer warrior. I always shared with her about the guys I was dating, and I valued her perspective. I told her a guy had come into the office today. We hit it off talking. He had just gotten his master's degree, he was on fire for Jesus, and he used to be gay, and I thought I might want to go out with him...

Now, since I had been open to dating many different guys, that meant I was currently seeing a few who were not so deep in their walks with Christ. When my mom heard Jim was "on fire for Jesus," that positively struck her, and she said, "I think you should go out with him." That was the "permission" I needed, any hesitancy went away, and I was free to go out with Jim.

He called me the next day, and we went out for coffee. As we talked, even on our first date, I kept seeing that we had significant life values in common. When we hugged goodbye that night, I felt the spark of romance and noticed how strong his arms were around me.

Jim was a strong leader and respected at church, and we soon fell in love. Four months after our first coffee date, we became engaged, and five months after that, we were married.

TWO HEARTS JOINED

My gay background did not scare Amanda. She had her share of questions, but I always kept the lines of communication open. A few weeks into our relationship, there was a critical event that would forge our relationship and serve as a foreshadow for some of the future adversity we would face.

The date was November 4, 2008, and it was the night Barack Obama won the U.S. presidential election. By this point, I was an active participant in politics and did whatever I could to stand up for Biblical principles—such as the sanctity of marriage.

Under California state law, the people of the state have the freedom to add initiatives, change or add a law, and even change the state's constitution. In a rare move, the people of California sponsored an initiative (known as Proposition 8) to change California's Constitution with these 14 words, "Only marriage between a man and a woman is valid or recognized in California."

As the election results came in that night, it became apparent that the Republican party would lose the national election. Miraculously though, the Prop 8 initiative was going to pass—a win for man-woman marriage. I was invited to the Orange County headquarters to celebrate the success, and I invited Amanda to come with me.

When news of the proposition's passing was announced, Amanda and I celebrated—she in her quiet and dignified manner, and I jumped around and shouted for joy. As we said our goodbyes that night, she leaned forward for our first kiss. In her typical good humor, she said it was a good thing she had called things off with the other guys she was seeing because she had been wanting to kiss me! We laughed, and I knew that night she was mine for good.

I went to bed on top of the world. This lady with the heart of God and Jesus in her eyes was now my girlfriend, and we had just won the most significant (and the most expensive) state initiative in history.[20]

But the next morning, Amanda and I had a rude awakening. Members of the media had captured our celebration on camera, and before we knew it, our faces were featured on the *LA Times, Chicago Tribune, Orange County Register,* and even a number of foreign-based papers.

I remember calling Amanda on her drive to work, ecstatic about all the publicity we received. She shared my excitement, but as soon as I hung up the phone, the storm hit. Horrible phone calls, death threats, harassment, and warnings of harm to Amanda and me began rolling in. It got pretty bad, and both of our employers took steps to protect us.

While another type of girl might have thought she made a mistake getting into a relationship with someone who caused this amount of backlash, Amanda held firm, and we weathered the storm together. An event that could have been a deal breaker for others proved to be a forging moment in our relationship.

THE RING

By Christmas of 2008, I knew it was only a matter of time before I would ask Amanda to marry me.

My parents were living in the Midwest and I was visiting them over the holidays. After we opened up all of the Christmas gifts that day and all of the nieces and nephews had gone to bed, my mom said, "I think there is one more gift that hasn't been opened." She pulled out a simply wrapped box with no card or writing, handed it to me, and told me to open it.

I did, and to my surprise, there was a diamond ring. It was the ring my dad bought for my mom when he proposed to her. It was beautiful, and the marquis-cut .52-karat diamond sparkled like I'd never seen before. It had been on Mom's original wedding band next to the engagement band, and the ring was designed to interlock the engagement and wedding bands. My dad had taken it to a local jeweler to get it restored, cleaned, and polished to pass on as a family heirloom.

"Jim, it's yours," my mom said. "Your dad and I want you to have this to use when you propose to Amanda!"

Tears began running down my face as I gave my mom a hug and kiss. We had all been through a lot together, and that moment felt a bit like a pro athlete receiving a trophy. It wasn't just the physical jewelry that meant so much. It was all of the previous years of pain and heartache that made that moment possible.

It was also amazing because I had just purchased my first home, and had no money to spare. I had been wondering how I was going to buy a ring, and once again, God provided in an amazing way!

Two months later on February 6, 2009, I contacted Amanda's supervisor and asked if she could leave work after lunch on Friday. She had a work meeting with all of the directors at the graduate center at a restaurant called Il Forno Cafe. I contacted the restaurant owners, so they knew what I was doing. They let me come in early and place rose petals on the table.

When Amanda walked into the restaurant, she thought her boss had gone to unusual lengths to decorate the table so nicely for their work meeting. I soon made my grand entrance, and when I got down on one knee, we suddenly had the attention of the entire restaurant on us. I had a lengthy speech prepared, but in that moment, I lost it. The only words I could think to say were,

> God can take a chance meeting—a divine mistake—and turn it into something wonderful.

"Will you marry me?" To my relief, she said "Yes," and I slipped the family ring on her finger. I still get choked up when I think of that moment.

The year that followed was a whirlwind. Four months after my first coffee date with this beautiful girl, we were engaged. Five months after that in July 2009, we were married.

When I first met Amanda, I felt like heaven and earth collided. As my dad has always said, "Amanda is God's gift from heaven!" I couldn't agree more, and that old phrase remains true—*Do not settle for less. Wait for God's best.* It is only through waiting that we see how God can take a chance meeting—a divine mistake—and turn it into something wonderful.

CHAPTER 13

Restoring the Years
the Locusts Had Eaten

Even before we were married, Amanda and I had lengthy conversations about the way we would parent our kids. There was much to talk about.

We were convinced about the importance of being present for our children. Nothing can replace time, so we made the decision that one of us would stay home and serve as a full-time parent while the other one worked.

Both of us had master's degrees, but Amanda had long felt a desire in her heart to be a stay-at-home mom. On our first date, I had shared that I was very supportive of this and wanted the same thing for my future family. We knew cutting our income in half would take some planning, so we decided to do a test run for a year before we had children by living off only my salary and putting Amanda's earnings in savings. This turned out to be a wise move and showed us the strategy was possible.

In 2014, our first daughter was born, and Amanda made the transition from full-time working wife to full-time mom. In 2016, we added a baby boy to the mix and then another girl in 2018.

After all I had been through, the joy of having children was a surreal experience. Those moments directly after their births were special. As I held each one of them close to my chest, they became a real part of my restoration process. Seeing the joy in my parents' eyes was also healing. For years, they assumed this day would never happen, and the look on their smiling faces was priceless.

> The years the locusts had stolen from my life were being restored in incredible ways.

The years the locusts stolen from my life were being restored in incredible ways. God was writing a new chapter of redemption in my life's story, and I stood back in amazement at how He took what I thought was a mistake (my same-sex attraction) and turned it into a catalyst to grow the relationships I had with my wife, my kids, and my parents.

HOW MY SSA BENEFITED OUR MARRIAGE

While I would not want to relive my time in the gay community, I began to see how God redeemed this season to make me a better husband and parent. Amanda would say the same. There are a couple of reasons why this was the case.

For starters, my same-sex attraction (SSA) prompted me to seek out wise counselors. Before I met Amanda, I was under the realization that I might spend the rest of my life alone in celibacy. That wasn't my first option, but I was okay with it. I did not need someone else to complete me. God was enough. I believe the best marriages are not formed through a need to be completed but the desire to fulfill God's intended design. It's two individuals running toward Jesus, looking to the side, seeing one another, and locking arms to run the race together.

Another advantage was the network of healthy men I had around me. Because I was aware of my added need for male role models, I was surrounded with a solid group of guys who kept me grounded.

Along with this, my five-year journey in a sinful lifestyle helped me know my limitations. I knew what I could and could not handle. There were no secret sins I kept back from Amanda. Everything was out in the open from the beginning.

In the words of Amanda—*I know I am the first woman Jim has been intimate with, and that makes me feel free from comparison. I have such peace knowing I am the only one for Jim.*

How could Jim's past be an answer to my own prayer? Because God can turn a mistake into something for His glory. After we were married, Jim would tell me there is nothing better than physical intimacy the way God intended. And I can testify that the physical closeness we experience as man and wife is very fulfilling to both of us.

> The best marriages are not formed through a need to be completed but the desire to fulfill God's intended design. It's two individuals running toward Jesus, looking to the side, seeing one another, and locking arms to run the race together.

When Jim shares his testimony publicly, I am often reminded of all of Jim's past experiences with his same-sex attraction. I forget Jim's past because it is not a part of our everyday life. We have the normal struggles of any marriage. Big struggles like making hard financial decisions and little struggles like when we can't agree on what furniture to get for our house.

We also have the normal frustrations of families with young kids like not having enough alone time or not getting as much sleep as we might like. But I have seen how Jim's struggle and deliverance from same-sex-attraction has informed our parenting to make us stronger.

HOW MY SSA BENEFITED OUR PARENTING

Amanda and I are on the same page when it comes to parenting. We share almost identical worldviews, so we believe the same on all of the major issues.

Because I missed out on the opportunity to connect with my dad in my youth, it makes me more intentional to experience those bonding moments with my son. Instead of focusing on my to-do list each day, I pause and take time to play Legos or read him a bedtime book on trains. Amanda and I have worked together to make sure my son bonds with me in heathy ways.

As she shares—*I know that Jim's connection with our son has to be different than mine. I may not understand why daddy "plays rough" or jokes around about things like burping, but I step aside for Jim to have space for male bonding with our son. I encourage these things, even if I don't always understand them.*

Jim will occasionally give up his morning gym workout for extra snuggle time with just daddy and the kids. These sacrifices come from a place of Jim wanting to reach his kids and do something meaningful with them. It is something all good dads will do, and Jim's dependence on God makes him want to be a good dad to our kids.

Jim has experienced the deep forgiveness of God, so he is quick to ask forgiveness of our kids (and me) when it is needed. Jim is an example and true leader to me and the kids in how he asks for forgiveness.

WHAT IT MEANS TO LOVE MY FAMILY

Along with my shift in becoming a man came a shift in my perspective of healthy relationships. Rewind several years to when Amanda and I were about to be married. She thought it would be good for us to go to premarital counseling. I told her I had already been through tons of counseling sessions and did not need it, but she said this was important to her. So I decided to go, and I'm glad I did.

During one of our meetings, Steve (whom I previously mentioned was the husband of my female high school youth pastor Cori and mentor when I came back to Christ) taught us the three Ps of good decision making in a relationship—provide, protect, and promote. I liked these so much that I even added a fourth one, pleasure. To this day, whenever I make decisions, I ask myself the question, *Will this activity provide, protect, promote, or bring pleasure to my family?*

Take work for instance. I love what I do! God created me to do what I'm doing—He's wired me for Church United (ChurchUnited.com), helping pastors engage in government at the local, state, and federal levels. I'm a pastor to pastors. Before going away for a business trip, I check my motives and make sure the trip is going to promote the best interests of my family. And then there are those trips to the beach with my family that bring them great pleasure. As time has passed, I have gotten to the place where I seldom think through this process. I do it instinctively.

Even as I worked on this section of the book, a specific example came up. It was afternoon time, and my kids were itching to go to the local swimming pool that day. But I was on a roll and getting stuff done. If it was up to me, I would have stayed home and worked on this chapter and all of the other things I needed to accomplish. But thinking through the four Ps, it was an easy decision to take the break and spend some time with my family.

WORKING TOGETHER AS A TEAM

My years as a single man meant there were many selfish tendencies I needed to overcome. I was used to living life alone and now there was another person in the picture. But the big pieces of the puzzle were in place. I was committed to change and growth.

My relationship with Amanda was going to be a team partnership. We would make decisions together. For example, Amanda and I are on the same page when it comes to disciplining our kids. I don't have one standard and then she comes along with another. We work together. When one of our kids does something wrong, we respond with, "Oh no, this is so sad!" That is our kids' cue they are in trouble and need to change their tune, or their actions will result in a time-out.

My kids have no idea I was a Former homosexual. It's not a part of my married or family life. They know I share my story at churches and work with pastors. We have decided to introduce LGBTQ topics to our kids at an age appropriate level and from scripture. With our oldest child being age 7, right now we talk about how God designed families with man-woman marriage and how God designed our bodies. At these ages we focus on having comfortable conversations where they are free to share with us and we respond to their questions.

MALE AND FEMALE ROLES

I admit my background has led to some hypersensitivity when it comes to male and female roles, but I want my kids to know men are men and women are women. Period.

I want my children to understand God created them with a penis or a vagina. Both are good. Both are wonderful. One is male. One is female. My two-year-old knows the difference. My four-year-old knows the difference. My seven-year-old knows the difference.

For example, my son was playing with his sisters and decided to goof off and put on one of their dresses. I think he just liked the color. I told him, "Son, boys don't do that. They wear firemen and policemen uniforms—not dresses." Later that day, the yellow princess dress he liked magically disappeared, and in its place, some new masculine dress-up clothes arrived in the mail.

Initially, Amanda wasn't so sure about my decision. She thought I overreacted. And she was probably right. We agreed that we didn't want our boy to feel bad over just playing a game, but it was still very important to us that we taught him the differences between what it meant to be male and female.

In Amanda's words, *I realized our son needed both my perspective and Jim's perspective. He needed my perspective to gently try to redirect him away from the princess dress, and he needed Jim as his daddy to explain how a man would do it. Now that I'm looking back on this situation that happened several years ago, I can see that Jim connected with our son by role-modeling for him. It was a powerful moment. Our son wants to be like his daddy and hasn't asked to put on the dress again because it is more fun to dress up like daddy showed him.*

Amanda and I joke about our parenting styles, and she has come up with this phrase, "Mommy Milk and Daddy Fun!" She is so supportive and regularly tells me how she sees me being a good dad."

THE IMPORTANCE OF INTENTIONALITY

When it comes to parenting, I'm very intentional to love each of my children as God created them. My goal is to encourage their gifts, talents, desires, and dreams. I love individually taking my girls on daddy-daughter dates and taking my son on daddy-son adventures.

If you are a parent who has not built much of a connection with your kids, I want to encourage you that it is never too late to start. My dad and I began our new relationship when I was 28, and it continues to this day at age 48—20 years of intentionally building relationship and growing deeper in respect, admiration, counsel, experience, and wisdom. I've learned to appreciate these characteristics and qualities in my dad. I even took my dad to a Division 1 college football game—not for me—but him and my son!

> Do one thing today that will build a point of connection between you and your son.

Watching my dad connect with my children is so rewarding. He is a great papa to our kids, and I've been able to see my dad in a whole new light. There have been times he has opened up and shared how he was impatient and too harsh with me and my siblings growing up. My mom loves to spoil and dote on our children, and it's been wonderful to see each child uniquely connect with their grandma. It's been wonderful to continue my relationship with my mom and watch that growth dynamic increase my love and gratefulness.

All of this took time. Right now, the vision might seem like a fantasy for you and your son. That's okay. Just take it one day at time. There is a phrase I like that goes like this, *Do the next right thing.* Don't focus on recovering 15 years of a broken relationship in one afternoon. Instead, do one thing today that will build a point of connection between you and your son.

CHAPTER 14

The Battle Never Ends

Soon after my initial return to Christ, I took what some might consider to be an extreme step. I contacted my cousin who had faced a tough background of her own and asked her to give me a hand. There were still remnants of my gay past, and I knew the Holy Spirit wanted them out of my life. He brought to mind a pair of black leather chaps and some other gear I still owned that had been what I wore during my days in the gay community.

She and I took these items to a nearby beach and set them on fire. Again, to some this might have seemed like a crazy step, but I knew it was important to remove any reminders of the life I used to live.

While that moment, along with a few others, served as a defining point in my spiritual journey, I will be the first to say the battle was far from over. To this day, I view myself as more of a *contender* than a *champion*. Yes, I have victory through Christ, but each day is a fight against evil as I seek to put Christ's kingdom purposes ahead of my own (Ephesians 2:10-20).

As a public speaker who now has the opportunity to rub shoulders with Christians of all different backgrounds, there is a common thread that holds different denominational backgrounds together. It is this idea of what we might call "quick redemption." We love to hear stories about how God has worked in people's lives and how He has transformed their behavior in the process. We eat up stories like the alcoholic who met Jesus and is now sober or the gang member who said goodbye to a life of drugs and theft and is now a strong Christian leader in the church community.

From a personal perspective, Christians love a narrative that goes something like this, *Here is Jim Domen. He used to be gay. Now look at him! He has a wife and kids. This could be your story!*

> Temptation is all around us, and my periodic moments of same-sex attraction are just one of many desires I resist. It is my response to these temptations that tells the real story.

But what few people besides Amanda understand is the constant battle that continues. Yes, my SSA has diminished over time, but there are still moments when I am tempted. Just as there are times I struggle with opposite-sex temptations, there are points I struggle with same-sex temptations. The war never stops. I have freedom, but I still have to fight.

There are moments I might come across something that takes my mind to a dark place or triggers a memory from my past that I would rather forget. In these moments, I call out to the Holy Spirit for help.

I have struggled with lust, porn, and viewing inappropriate content. Even since being married to Amanda, there have been a few times when I messed up and sinned by looking at something I should have avoided. But even in those moments of regression, God was good. I knew this was not the life I wanted to live, and my confession to Him and Amanda brought restoration.

Temptation is all around us, and my periodic moments of same-sex attraction are just one of many desires I resist. Every day I face temptations to be angry, dishonest, proud, and arrogant. I could cheat on taxes, speak harshly to my wife, or become impatient with my kids. These are all temptations I face, but my temptations do not define who I am. It is my response to these temptations that tells the real story.

Just as temptation to steal does not make one a thief, temptation to act out with someone of the same sex does not make someone gay. Acting on a temptation is when it becomes sinful.

Author C.S. Lewis famously stated, "A man who gives in to temptation after five minutes simply does not know what it would have been like an hour later. That is why bad people, in one sense, know very little about badness—they have lived a sheltered life by always giving in. We never find out the strength of the evil impulse inside us until we try to fight it; and Christ, because He was the only man who never yielded to temptation, is also the only man who knows to the full what temptation means—the only complete realist."[21]

This was my story.

During the five years I gave in to my same-sex desires, life was easy. The war was over because I had surrendered in defeat. It was only when I reengaged and started fighting back that I noticed the true darkness of evil and the full power of Christ.

> It was only when I reengaged and started fighting back that I noticed the true darkness of evil and the full power of Christ.

The Cycle of Sin

John 3:19-20

1 John 2:15-17
Psalm 38:4; 69:5;
32:5

James 1:13-15

Phil. 3:18-19
Psalm 4:2;
25:2-4, 20
Prov. 18:3
Rom. 10:11

2 Cor. 10:5b

H
A
L
T
S
D

© 2001 Ricky P. Chelette, Minister of Single Adults/Outreach First Baptist Church,
Arlington, TX ricky.chelette@fbca.org; Living Hope Ministries www.livehope.org for
online support forums for youth, adults, and friends and family.

THE CYCLE OF SIN

The longer you resist, the more you begin to notice patterns. You begin to see how different settings, times of the day, or life situations can make you especially vulnerable to temptation. As I went through the early days of this struggle, a spiritual coach of mine introduced me to Pastor Ricky Chelette's six emotion triggers that can often be gateways to a dark place. The emotions that should cause you to be cautious are when you feel:

- Hungry
- Angry
- Lonely
- Tired
- Stressed
- Depressed

Any time I sense one of these emotions in myself, it is a prime opportunity for the enemy to gain a foothold in my life. It's here that I do as 2 Corinthians 10:5 instructs and "take every thought captive."

A practical way I do this is through "packing my gym bag." As someone who enjoys working out and competing in Ironman competitions, I have spent my fair share of hours in the gym or outdoor training. I noticed that during these times, there were moments when thoughts of lust might transpire. These came in the forms of both same-sex and opposite-sex attractions.

It was after one of these moments that God grabbed my attention. I was doing some reading through James 1 when I came across verses 13-15:

> *When tempted, no one should say,*
> *"God is tempting me." For God cannot be tempted by evil,*
> *nor does he tempt anyone; but each person is tempted when they*
> *are dragged away by their own evil desire and enticed.*
> *Then, after desire has conceived, it gives birth to sin; and sin,*
> *when it is full-grown, gives birth to death.*

"Dragged away by their own evil desire." That was my problem! My real challenge wasn't the man or woman running next to me on the treadmill. It was my mindset going into this workout. Was I going into it with a mind ready to lust or a mind committed to focusing on God?

> I had to win the battle in my mind before I had a chance of resisting with my body.

This passage helped me see my real battle started each morning when I packed my gym bag. It was already won or lost by the time I arrived at the gym. I had to win the battle in my mind before I had a chance of resisting with my body. This is where I needed to fight to break the sin cycle.

As humans, our temptation is to ponder, dwell on, and think about sins we would like to commit. And then, after we justify our actions, we seek to medicate our broken condition with something that numbs the pain of guilt we feel inside.

At any point, the opportunity to jump off the sin cycle is there. But because sin is pleasurable in the moment, it often takes an intervention of God to help someone break free.

Now that I am a parent, I know the pain it causes when my children push me to the side and take what Amanda or I do for granted. I find myself thinking, *Why, you selfish little child!* Then I pause and remember all God has done for me and those many times I rejected what He offered in pursuit of my own desires.

Why do I do this? John 3:19-20 provides the answer:

This is the verdict: Light has come into the world, but people loved darkness instead of light because their deeds were evil. Everyone who does evil hates the light, and will not come into the light for fear that their deeds will be exposed.

This is the real fear we have that keeps us going through the sin cycle. We fear what might happen if our true motives were exposed. I know this has been my story. It is not just the embarrassment of confessing a sin that prevents me from making things right with God, but it is the growing realization of the true state of my heart. I sense the guilt, shame, and weight of my failure. And as this happens, I come back to my only hope in 1 John 2:15-17:

Do not love the world or anything in the world.
If anyone loves the world, love for the Father is not in them.
For everything in the world—the lust of the flesh, the lust
of the eyes, and the pride of life—comes not from the Father but
from the world. The world and its desires pass away,
but whoever does the will of God lives forever.

This is the great hope we have as believers. We will live forever. But the reality is that in our present state of living in a broken world, we always face the temptation to get back on the sin cycle. Our focus becomes skewed, and we see the temporal as most important and the eternal as something that holds little significance. I'm reminded of a lecture I heard from brilliant scholar and USC philosopher Dallas Willard, "Live as eternity is now."

> That is why the greatest opportunity to resist temptation is in the beginning stages of a temptation when we "pack our gym bags."

That is why the greatest opportunity to resist temptation is in the beginning stages of a temptation when we "pack our gym bags."

TEN STEPS TO FREEDOM

Over the years of counseling primarily men, I have helped them become victorious by implementing what I call *Ten Steps to Freedom*. If you have a child who wants to break free of acting out on his or her same-sex desires, this is a great place to start.

I have used these steps with multiple men I counsel, many with same-sex attraction, opposite-sex attraction, or issues with pornography. It's intense and requires commitment, but it has proven to be very effective.

Step 1: Daily Bible Reading and Prayer

This is basic, but it is critical. Few professing Christians read their Bibles and pray in such a way that they expect God to show up and transform their lives.

The goal is not to read and pray just as a habit of discipline. Instead, the real reason every follower of Christ should read their Bible and pray is so they can become more like Christ in the process.

Step 2: Regular Accountability

Some men need daily accountability, while others might need it a couple times a week. But if you or someone you love is in the process of breaking free from sexual addiction, you need godly men around you who will challenge you and encourage you to grow.

Because the weight of dealing with same-sex attraction can be difficult for one accountability partner to handle, I encourage the men I counsel to find multiple people to journey with them. The more people you can have on your team, the more strength you will receive.

Step 3: Meet with Other Men (They Do Not Need to Be Former Homosexuals) Who Have Overcome SSA and Are Still Struggling

You need other guys who are fighting with you, and then you need those people who model healthy masculinity in your life. Don't make the mistake I made in graduate school and latch on to one person, thus creating an unhealthy relationship. Again, it's in the *multitude* of counselors where there is safety. Remember the "Rule of Three"—when traveling or meeting together, three is a safer number than one on one.

Step 4: Get Involved in a Good Church

Hebrews 10:25 reminds us not to forsake the assembling of ourselves together. Even though I experienced my early share of frustration in the church, the strength and support I have received from other people of faith has been critical for the spiritual development of my soul.

Step 5: Find a Men's Accountability Group

It all comes back to relationships. You want people in your life who know your struggles. As you hear other guys share about their battles with lust, being a good father, or putting God in front of their careers, you will discover you are not alone.

Instead of only thinking about *your* journey and *your* struggle, open yourself up and start caring for the needs of others.

Step 6: Go Through *The Steps to Freedom in Christ*

Author Neil Anderson wrote a fantastic book titled *The Steps to Freedom in Christ*.[22] In this book, he outlines seven steps I have found to be helpful:

- Step 1: Counterfeit versus Real
- Step 2: Deception versus Truth
- Step 3: Bitterness versus Forgiveness
- Step 4: Rebellion versus Submission
- Step 5: Pride versus Humility
- Step 6: Bondage versus Freedom
- Step 7: Curses versus Blessings

Out of all of my *Ten Steps to Freedom*, this is the one I think is most important. Going through this book is one of the most effective ways to deal with someone's past and the current issues they may be facing. I ask men to block out four-hour timeframes. We take as many as needed to finish the seven steps.

Step 7: Identify Your Key Triggers

Go back to Ricky Chelette's six triggers and ask yourself, *When am I most triggered to act out on my temptations? Is it when I am hungry, angry, lonely, tired, stressed, or depressed?*

Step 8: Go Through Desert Stream Ministries

This is one of the best resources I can recommend. If you or someone you love struggles with same-sex attraction, desertstream.org is a great place to get help.

Desert Stream Ministries has helped me tremendously. It was founded by Andrew Comiskey in 1980. Andrew was a former homosexual man who has been married for over 40 years to his wife Annette. Originally, DSM only focused on homosexuality, but it has grown to cover multiple issues relating to fear, insecurity, marital problems, co-dependency, pornography, effects of abuse, poor boundaries, sexual addiction, promiscuity, isolation, the inability to trust, anger, forgiveness, masturbation, gender-identity issues, unwanted same-sex attraction, fantasy, shame, and self-hatred.

Step 9: Consider Going Through Sexaholics Anonymous

If someone is dealing with a more serious case of sex addiction, Sexaholics Anonymous can provide a deeper level of help that is tailored to individual needs.

Step 10: Find a Great Counselor

Great counselors look different for different people. Regardless, find someone who shares your values, knows what they are doing, and has credibility in their field. My counselor friend T is one of the main reasons I am where I am today.

As you consider the *Ten Steps to Freedom*, keep in mind they do not have to be done in any particular order. You might start with a counselor and work your way to the other steps from there. However, it is important that you get help, find other men to journey with you, and develop a deep level of relationship with Christ.

Only this will set you on the path to victory and freedom.

IT ALL COMES BACK TO A CHOICE

Whenever I speak, I always ask this question to those in attendance, "Who in this room has never been tempted?" I've never had anyone raise their hand. I remind the audience that Jesus was tempted in every way, yet He did not sin. Temptation does not equate to sin.

There is a reason I quote so much Scripture in this chapter—it is the key to winning the battle as did Jesus when He was tempted by the devil. Ephesians 6:10-14 states:

> *Finally, be strong in the Lord and in his mighty power.*
> *Put on the full armor of God, so that you can take your stand*
> *against the devil's schemes. For our struggle is not against*
> *flesh and blood, but against the rulers, against the authorities,*
> *against the powers of this dark world and against the spiritual*
> *forces of evil in the heavenly realms. Therefore put on the full*
> *armor of God, so that when the day of evil comes,*
> *you may be able to stand your ground, and after you*
> *have done everything, to stand. Stand firm then, with*
> *the belt of truth buckled around your waist, with the breastplate*
> *of righteousness in place, and with your feet fitted with*
> *the readiness that comes from the gospel of peace.*

Every day I need to put on the full armor. If I do not, I am vulnerable to attack. In this book, I have shared my best tips and pieces of advice, but every decision we make comes down to a choice—a choice to please self or please God.

> Every decision we make comes down to a choice—a choice to please self or please God.

Therapists have their place, spiritual leaders are essential, and being surrounded with great men is critical, but nothing can replace choice. Do what Deuteronomy 30 instructs and **CHOOSE LIFE**.

Parents, remember this—you can do everything you can to help your child flourish in their faith, but never forget that he has a choice. Do not place on your shoulders a burden you cannot bear. You can pray for your son, encourage him, and pay off his credit cards. But you cannot choose for him. That is a decision he alone must make.

CHAPTER 15

No Mistakes

It is often assumed there is a large percentage of the U.S. population that is gay. Some estimate this number is as high as 25%. In reality, the number is probably closer to about 3.8%.[23] For being such a relatively small portion of the American population, those in the gay community hold a powerful voice. November 2021, Barna released a poll that 30% of millennials identify as LGBTQ.[24]

The problem today is kids in public schools are indoctrinated to believe biology holds little value. A child might have every physical characteristic of being a male but choose to identify as female, bi-sexual, or transgender.

Unfortunately, society has shifted so much on this topic that those who question this line of thinking from a scientific perspective are viewed as bigots. "Gender identity is a choice," we are told.

BECOMING A CULTURAL FRAUD

Here is the problem for people like me who are same-sex attracted or have left homosexuality and choose to live within God's intended design for creation. We are told we do not exist. Many political leaders, many of whom do not experience same-sex attraction, believe the Jim Domens of the world are cultural frauds. They believe the great relationship I enjoy with my wife and three kids is a lie built on a false understanding of personal identity. If I were "true to myself,"

I would remain in the gay community. They do not know what to do with people like me.

A brief example of this comes from back in 2018 when Assemblyman Evan Low introduced Assembly Bill 2943 that proposed a change to business law making Sexual Orientation Change Efforts (SOCE) a fraudulent practice.

Any time money would be exchanged for counseling, purchase of books, materials, honorariums, or speaking engagements, it would be considered a fraudulent transaction in the state of California.

In May 2018, Church United sponsored and led former LGBTQ people to California's capitol to speak truth about this unjust bill. As a reporter from the *Associated Press* and a journalist from Sacramento's ABC news affiliate shared, they had never seen so many people come out to stop a bill from being passed.

AB 2943 passed the Senate Judiciary Committee and was voted on in both houses, the state senate and the state assembly. I was an expert witness and testified to the committee that my family—my wife and children (we had two children at the time)—were not frauds.

Prior to the Senate Committee Hearing, about 30 former LGBTQ people, including me, stood on the steps of California's capitol, telling their stories. I listened as they confessed what happened to their bodies and told horrible stories of sexual abuse, depression, and suicide. But as the bill was debated, they were metaphorically spilling the blood of Jesus over California's capitol as they told the miraculous stories of healing, redemption, and change.

Miraculously, on the last day of the legislature session, Assemblyman Evan Low withdrew this bill, even after it had passed the assembly and senate chambers. All it needed was

Governor Jerry Brown's signature (something that was sure to happen) and the bill would be signed into law.

What changed Low's mind was not some intellectual argument that moved him to change his beliefs. To the contrary, Low continues to hold similar views to this day. But what did happen was he heard a lot of stories. He saw the faces of men and women whom society had termed as "frauds," and this was what prompted him to change his mind. (I also believe God played a role in Assemblyman Low withdrawing his bill.)

Stories are the key to change. It starts with pastors preaching Biblical truth about human sexuality from pulpits, but that is not enough. We need to see real-life examples of men and women who actually experience same-sex desires but have also experienced the joy of living life as God designed.

NO MISTAKES

At the close of this book, I include stories of men and women who are Formers—gay, lesbian, and transgender but have experienced the grace of God in a life-changing way. One of the most dramatic of these stories comes from my friend Angel Colon who survived the Pulse Night Club Massacre in June 2016 after being shot seven times:

My life before I pursued change in my sexuality was what I would call "A Hot Mess." Lonely, empty, unhappy, shackled, and unloved were the ways I felt for eight years. The more unhappy I was, the worse it got. My life was so consumed by homosexuality, drugs, and liquor that I wouldn't give the time of day to my family. Having been raised in a strong Christian home, I felt a deep conflict between what I had known to be good and right and the life I was living. Even while being in the lifestyle, the Holy Spirit would always tug at my heart. I would have moments when I would weep while talking to Jesus and moments when I would be drunk in the club or party and start singing worship songs. Even living in the lifestyle, I always knew the Lord was calling out my name. I ignored those calls until the year 2016 when I was fed up with my life. I had what I wanted, who I wanted, but no happiness, real love or peace.

I woke up hung over after a night of drinking and drug use. That evening, I ended up at Pulse Gay Nightclub in Orlando, and 2:02 a.m. is when everything changed. Saying our goodbyes, we heard the first big POP! I dropped my drink, realizing the sounds were gunshots. As we ran, I was shot several times. I fell down, pulling my friends with me. As I was struggling to stand back up, I felt a footstep behind my left leg and heard a loud snap which resulted in my left femur being broken. I couldn't move or even feel my legs, so I covered my head and stayed still.

What followed was chaos all around me. I started comforting the lady lying next to me, whispering to her to pretend to be dead. I looked at her and heard a loud shot. As her eyes shut, I couldn't believe I just witnessed her death. I was terrified I was next. Feeling the shooter behind me, I uttered what I thought would be my last prayer. Even in that terrible moment, the peace and hope of God flooded me. I heard a loud shot and felt my body jump up and down as I was being shot all over again. I thought I was dead. After several minutes, I started hearing cop radios. I raised my hands calling out, "Please come get me! I'm alive!"

As I recovered mentally, physically, and spiritually, I caught myself fighting with the Lord about my temptations through my process until one night I fell on my knees and surrendered. In my prayer I said, "Lord, I surrender. Take my struggles and temptations, but not only that, take my whole heart. Take everything of me!" At that moment, the Holy Spirit spoke to me and said, "Angel, that is all He wanted. He wanted all of you, not just bits and pieces."

At that moment, I realized I was focusing so much on my sin instead of focusing on the person who was in charge of transforming my life, Jesus. I prayed day and night to be straight when all along I needed my whole heart to be restored. I needed to focus on my relationship with Jesus and getting to know Jesus because he is the truth, and the truth shall set you free. That is how I was able to find true freedom and true identity. I can now wake up every morning and say, "I AM GOOD WITH GOD!"

My life today is a complete 180 from the life I had before. Feeling empty and lonely inside was slowly destroying me, but I now know what was needed to be fulfilled in my life, a true relationship with Jesus. I was able find out what true freedom was, and now the Lord has permitted for me to be one of the co-founders of Fearless Identity with my ministry partner Luis Ruiz as we share our stories to the world of what the Lord has done in our lives and help equip the Body of Christ in how to welcome the LGBTQ community with open arms because the harvest is coming back to Jesus Christ.

Now that I'm living in the Lord, I sure know that I am not a mistake and that everything that has happened in my process is all in His will. Not only has my life changed completely, but because of that change, I have been able to join others in their journeys of finding freedom and their identity in Christ as well as true peace, happiness, and love.

SOME OF THE TOUGH QUESTIONS I HEAR

While stories help touch a person's heart, truth is what sets a person free. This brings us to those tough conversations. How do you interact with a gay son who does not believe what he is doing is wrong? His story is not like Angel's, and he wants nothing to do with God and little to do with you.

Below are some of the most common questions I receive from parents in this position and my response to their questions.

Will My Gay Son Still Make It to Heaven?

This is a tough call, and the easy response is to say I am not the one who decides. When I was actively engaged in the gay community, I certainly thought the answer was yes. My philosophy was that I was saved and God would forgive me no matter what decisions I made. Since coming back to faith, my understanding of Hebrews 10:26-30 has led me to question this position.

I suppose the question ultimately points to one's view of salvation. Some might claim a "once saved, always saved" viewpoint. Others would suggest that I was always God's child and it was only a matter of time before I returned. And some would say I was lost. This is one of the great tensions of the gospel.

My encouragement to you, the parent, is to not make this question the focus of your prayers. Your focus should be on your son encountering the awesome wonder of Jesus Christ. Prior to my venture into the gay community, I thought that's where I was. But I was just a good boy who claimed Jesus as Savior. I had not surrendered to Christ as Lord. However, I still heard from God even in an actively gay life. I'd never admit it—but God never left me.

God Made Me This Way and He's OK with It!

God made you male (or female depending on a child's biological sex). You are not a mistake. You are God's design, but you can't be made whole apart from Christ.

Our sexuality connects to our environment, childhood and youth development, and psychological experiences with our parents or lack of parent(s). LGB is learned primarily in the early years of childhood when children are not cognizant of their sexual development, environment, and effects on their sexuality. Many times when people express they were "born this way," it's because they had some dramatic sexual experience as a child or youth, and even if abuse was not an issue, it feels like you were "always this way." There is no biological evidence, nor is there some gene or genetic marker that makes someone LGB. Sex confusion (Transgender) is a psychological issue not explicitly related to lesbian, gay, or bisexual.

Because the development of our sexuality is influenced by outside factors (like environment, psychological development, connection with our parents, etc.), those factors can also distort our sexuality. It happens at such a young age that we don't remember it, meaning it feels like we are "born this way." The LGB sexual expression follows a different path than God intended.

Should I Attend My Gay Son's Wedding?

This question is fresh in my memory. I had dinner just last night with a couple friends, and one of them shared their daughter has been in a lesbian marriage in another state. They are often asked if they went to their child's wedding. It is a common question parents of gay children receive, and any answer but yes will surely lead some to believe they are homophobic.

Here is my response whenever I am asked if I would attend a gay friend's wedding. First, as a pastor, I would never officiate a gay, lesbian, or any other form of marriage different from a male and female union. As a Christian, marriage is not a union defined by government. It is defined by God. Marriage, as He defines it, is between one man and one woman. Officiating any other form of marriage would be leading those in attendance away from truth and thus away from God.

The next question of whether or not to attend your child's wedding does not have such a cut-and-dried answer. A couple of notes ... first, both parents need to seek the Holy Spirit and determine what would be best for them and their child. Parents, you should have a unified front and come to your decision together. It might be you do not attend the actual ceremony, but you attend the reception. I would recommend not attending either event.

Again, the answer is not always the same as you seek to offer truth in love.

What About the Holidays?

Every holiday I get this question from parents, aunts, uncles, and other relatives. What should we do? Either the family who is hosting the event inquires or a family member is asking advice if they should go because their gay brother and his partner will be there. We have kids, they don't know about their uncle, or we don't want them to think we are supporting their behavior.

As I've shared, I am grateful for my parents' clear and strong boundaries. Although I raged at them and questioned their Christianity and their walk with Jesus, it was what I needed when I came home. A safe home, clear boundaries, a sanctuary of truth for my restoration. I know too many families who have completely embraced their son and partner only to be completely cut off years down the road because they still held God's design for human sexuality. However, sometimes the Holy Spirit might lead you and your spouse to a different conclusion. Yes, you're the uncle and aunt—not the parents—invite them over, love on them, and help guide your family and extended family on your reasoning. It's a great teaching point. I'll never forget Rosario Butterfield's sharing of how a Christian neighbor invited her and her lesbian partner over for dinner. Guess what? It led her to seeing and following Jesus and changing her life.

What Is the Homosexual Agenda?

Have you heard of this phrase? I know I've used it in conferences and other forms of communication. I remember reading a comment from a gay man that asked, "What's this homosexual agenda I keep hearing about? It's not like a bunch of homosexual men get together and plot to take over the society." He is correct. When I have used the phrase "Homosexual Agenda," I equate it to a spiritual movement of dark forces advancing a plan that is contrary to God's will and His plan for humanity. It's in direct opposition to what is best for humanity.

It's an unprecedented cultural shift that has taken root in the United States, the United Kingdom, and Australia which has been transforming the globe in a direction away from God's design for humanity. Frankly, it's been a brilliant strategy that has continued to deceive and trick humanity into believing the narrative of old, "Did God really say that?"

What Pronoun Should We Use?

There are only two sexes, male and female. My advice would be to join a person where they are, but you always want to point them to truth. You may not even know you're talking with a woman who is biologically a man or a man who is biologically a woman.

What is LGBTQ+∞?

Lesbian, Gay, Bisexual, Transgender, Queer or Questioning, and the plus symbol implies whatever anyone perceives their sexuality may be. The infinity symbol (∞) notes the options are endless.

Queer and Questioning are interchangeable. Many have asked me, "But isn't 'queer' a derogatory word?" This depends on the context. Many in the LGBTQ community call themselves queer, but if someone is using the term in a belittling way, I would refrain from using the word queer.

What Terminology Should I Use?

This depends on the individual. For example, some would not like it that I use the phrases "gay lifestyle" or "homosexual agenda." Others couldn't care less. Personally, I stick to 1 Corinthians 6:9-11 and use the word "Former" to describe myself and others who have left the LGBTQ lifestyle. I am a Former. I was Formerly a gay man, but that is no longer my identity. I am now a Christian, a Christ follower, and it is in Him my true identity lies. May I ask you this question, "What type of Former were you prior to coming to Christ?"

My suggestion is do your best to understand who you are speaking to and be sensitive to their preferences. There is no need to unnecessarily offend someone to prove a point. Always remember your goal is to help them see Jesus, not push an agenda.

A GOD OF NO MISTAKES

If you have asked yourself some of those questions, you know what it means to feel the weight they carry. The questions are not asked merely to gain more information. They are asked from a heart in the midst of tremendous hurt.

Many Christians, including those who do not have friends in the gay community, do not know what to do when it comes to questions about issues such as same-sex marriage. They feel it is unloving, exclusive, and judgmental to stand for truth, so little by little they cave to the will of mainstream culture.

Today, as the founder and CEO of Church United, I believe God has called me to help transform the world for Christ by disrupting pastors, uniting the Church, and trans-forming our communities. It is to this I have devoted my life.

My heart aches for parents in your situation, yet time and time again I have witnessed that we serve a God of no mistakes. As we stand for truth and love those God has called us to love, He can take any hard situation and accomplish the impossible. He can take a nightclub massacre and create a disciple, and He can take the ruins of that broken relationship you have with your son and do the impossible.

CHAPTER 16

Dear Parent

In the summer of 2021, the San Francisco Gay Men's Choir came out with a song they called a joke:

You think we're sinful
You fight against our rights
You say we all lead lives you can't respect
But you're just frightened
You think that we'll corrupt your kids
If our agenda goes unchecked
Funny, just this once, you're correct

We'll convert your children
Happens bit by bit
Quietly and subtly
And you will barely notice it
You can keep them from disco
Warn about San Francisco
Make 'em wear pleated pants
We don't care
We'll convert your children
We'll make them tolerant and fair[25]

While this song was intended to provide comedic relief, it outlines the belief many in that culture have. They believe those who do not support same-sex marriages are homophobic and dangerous to a civilized society. They see them as unreasonable, old fashioned, and bigoted.

If you are a Christian parent of a gay son, it places you in a position of immense guilt. Not only do you feel the weight of whom your son has become, but you also feel the pressure to accept and celebrate his coming out.

These can lead to some dark days. It might even feel as though a death in your family has occurred.

WHEN YOUR DREAMS DIE

Amanda and I have journeyed through our share of dark valleys together. The darkest days included the loss of our two babies at 16 and 14 weeks of pregnancy. My wife has given birth five times, but we only have three children.

Our first daughter, baby Samantha, still had a heartbeat at 16 weeks of life when Amanda's amniotic sac ruptured and all fluid was lost for some unknown reason, and our baby girl could not survive at such an undeveloped state of life. Two pregnancies later, we said goodbye to our baby boy Shane when the same thing happened again, this time after only 14 weeks. The first loss was the most devasting life issue I have ever encountered.

What was supposed to be a joyous occasion was cut short, leaving a broken father and mother to pick up the pieces of a life snuffed out too soon. It was such a dark day when we left the hospital with no baby in our arms. Everything about that time felt so wrong. Pregnant women were supposed to visit hospitals to *deliver* babies and then come home to raise them into adulthood. That is the circle of life. But for our first and third pregnancies, we came home with nothing. When my wife's milk came in, she had no baby to nurse. We were devastated.

Both of us were working full time, Amanda at a Christian university and I as a pastor. Thankfully, we had some amazing people around us who cried, brought us meals, and sent sympathy flowers. As time passed and the miscarriage was in our rearview mirror, it still took a long time for the pain to fade. People did not know what to say, and we did our best to cover up the hurt we felt inside.

The week after baby Samantha's death, I was grieving with Amanda in the silence of our home. I remembered thinking to myself, *God, why does everything have to be so painful? Why did I have to deal with same-sex attraction? Why did it take me till age 34 to be married? And now, why did you allow our first child to die?*

It is the "why" questions of life that will keep you up at night. My feeling of frustration at God shifted to those in the church. *God, no one cares about what I am going through,* I told Him. *They're all too focused on their joyous lives while my wife and I are sitting here in agony.*

Of course, none of that was true. People did care. But in moments of true agony, all you can feel is pain.

It wasn't until we lost baby Shane at 14 weeks that things started to change. I remember being parked at the Kaiser Hospital parking lot, sobbing my eyes out, when I took a call from my friend, Bishop Kevin Vann of the Catholic Orange County Dioceses.

Looking back, that was a divine appointment. I poured my heart out to Kevin, and he encouraged me and my wife to hold a memorial service to celebrate the life of our baby. "It will help you process the grief, bring closure, and celebrate the life God gave you," he said. A few days later, Bishop Vann came to our home and did a service around our kitchen table. I handmade a casket out of wood pieces and laid baby Shane's body in it, nestled in a hand-sewn blanket put together by a wonderful team of volunteers at the hospital. Shane had a little face, teeny tiny fingernails, and delicate hands, arms, joints, elbows, legs, and feet. His entire body fit in the palm of my hand, and yet he was perfectly formed. Bishop Vann was right, even in our pain it did help to honor and celebrate our tiny baby's life.

It is here that I go back to those thoughts from my friend Joe Dallas and his point about there being a death of expectations.[26] When your son comes out as gay, every expectation you had for him seems to go out the window, leaving you with a deep sense of loss.

Rather than cover up these emotions, lean into them. In the words of John Piper, "Weep deeply over the life that you hoped would be. Grieve the losses. Feel the pain. Then wash your face, trust God, and embrace the life that he's given you."[27]

As much as I despised all that came with the tragic loss of my two children, those times helped me understand life in a way that an existence free from pain could not. They taught me how to lament. I discovered that even in my darkest pain, God is present. God is here. God is with me. God is with my child. He will never leave or forsake me. God is God, and He is good.

THE POWER OF A PRAYING PARENT

As I neared this book's completion, I reached out to my mom, and she reminded me once again of the power of prayer. Being a parent, you might be tempted to think of prayer as a last resort. You may have tried everything else, but nothing seems to work.

It might be God is using this season of desperation to help you discover the real value of bringing your concerns to Him.

When I was away from God, below are some Scriptures my mom prayed over my life:

- Hebrews 4:12—"For the word of God is living and active. Sharper than any double-edged sword, it penetrates even to dividing soul and spirit, joints and marrow; it judges the thoughts and attitudes of the heart."
- John 14:13-14—"And I will do whatever you ask in my name, so that the Son may bring glory to the Father. You may ask me for anything in my name, and I will do it."
- Ephesians 3:14-21—"For this reason I kneel before the Father, from whom every family in heaven and on earth derives its name. I pray that out of his glorious riches he may strengthen you with power through his Spirit in your inner being, so that Christ may dwell in your hearts through faith. And I pray that you, being rooted and established in love, may have power, together with all the Lord's holy people, to grasp how wide and long and high and deep is the love of Christ, and to know this love that surpasses knowledge—that you may be filled to the measure of all the fullness of God."
- Philippians 1:3-6—"I thank my God every time I remember you. In all my prayers for all of you, I always pray with joy because of your partnership in the gospel from the first day until now, being confident of this, that he who began a good work in you will carry it on to completion until the day of Christ Jesus."
- Colossians 1:9-11—"For this reason, since the day we heard about you, we have not stopped praying for you. We continually ask God to fill you with the knowledge of his will through all the wisdom and understanding that the Spirit gives, so that you may live a life worthy of the Lord and please him in every way: bearing fruit in every good

work, growing in the knowledge of God, being strengthened with all power according to his glorious might so that you may have great endurance and patience."

- Matthew 7:7-8—"Ask and it will be given to you; seek and you will find; knock and the door will be opened to you. For everyone who asks receives; the one who seeks finds; and to the one who knocks, the door will be opened."

My encouragement to you is to make the Psalms your guidebook. Meditate on the words of David when he was in some of his most vulnerable states. Notice all of the passages in Scripture that highlight loss and offer hope.

DEAR PARENTS

I began this book with a note to my parents. Now, I want to address you, the reader—the parent who is hurting.

Dear Mom and Dad,

Your parenting is not a mistake. Your son is not a mistake. We live in a fallen world but have full access to the everlasting hope Jesus brings. For many years I asked the question, "Why? Why me?" God answered that question 34 years later. I do not know the timing of the questions you've asked, but I do know this—you are not alone.

I am encouraging you to press into God, just as the psalmist did in Psalm 46.

In Not a Mistake, I've only shared a handful of stories out of the thousands upon thousands of men and women who have chosen to change their lifestyle. Although "Formers" are a super minority, the global stories of transformation are interwoven such that skin color and race do not play contributing factors to

LGBTQ issues. Globally, we all deal with the same fallen nature, but you and I get to choose how we respond. Jesus came to save the sick, the dying, and the lost. Continue to model Jesus as you walk with your son. Never give up, and never forget change is possible. Your son is not a mistake.

Keep praying! God is faithful. He hears your cries and knows your pain.

Love,

Jim

Helpful Resources

The issues discussed in this book are unpacked in two programs—Living Waters and CrossCurrent.

As described on their website, Living Waters provides a thoughtful and safe place to look at the ways we've become ensnared. Through weekly times of worship, teaching, and small group prayer, our program leaders walk with participants in their struggle so they can live in freedom and truth. We pray for God's healing to restore broken areas of life so people can "love well" as God intended.

Living Waters is a 20-week closed group for men and women who are seeking healing in their lives. It is an intensive and unique small group. Ultimately, we learn how to press into Jesus more deeply, allowing Him to meet our needs and transform us for His kingdom purposes. With groups all over the world and with over 30 years of ministering God's healing love, the Living Waters program is a proven path of healing.

Through the worship, teaching, prayer, and small groups of Living Waters, we learn about God's powerful love for us and how Jesus is central to our hope for wholeness, the depths of our brokenness, our profound need for Him, and the power of the cross to restore our souls, sexuality, and relationship. Jesus is also the center of the process of walking out our healing, our place in the church, and loving others honorably.

CrossCurrent is an eight-week course where you meet once a week at a local church. CrossCurrent uses some of the same themes as the 20-week Living Waters group curriculum, but it condenses and simplifies the materials into an 8-week curriculum. CrossCurrent was originally designed as an introduction to the Living Waters program and is based on the same principles. Some churches use CrossCurrent as a starting point to bridge into a full Living Waters group. Other churches use CrossCurrent as a standalone study or an opportunity for evangelization with individuals who may be at the beginning stage of surrendering their whole person to Jesus Christ. Each meeting includes worship, prayer, and teachings. The eight teachings that make up CrossCurrent cover themes such as Getting Real: Jesus and the True Self, Getting Healed: How Jesus on the Cross Bears our Wounds, Becoming Secure in the Father's Love, and Beyond Brokenness.[28]

Family Support

LivingStonesMinistry.org – Support for family members dealing with loved ones with LGBTQ issues

Same-Sex Attraction (SSA) or Gender Confusion

CHANGEDMOVEMENT.com – Pastors Ken Williams (former homosexual) and Elizabeth Woning (former lesbian) at Bethel Church, Redding, California

DesertStream.org – Individuals dealing with LGBTQ or other sexual issues

ComingOutgain.com – Individuals dealing with SSA

TherapeuticChoice.com – Alliance for Therapeutic Choice and Scientific Integrity

SexChangeRegret.com – Sex Change Regret

FreedomToMarch.com – Freedom March

FearlessIdentity.co – Fearless Identity

PortlandFellowship.com – Portland, Oregon Fellowship

TRCRA.org.tw – Taiwan Rainbow Crosser Rights Association

Other People Who
Are Not a Mistake

April Lockhart
Los Angeles, California
United States
Age 40
Former Lesbian

Identifying and living as a lesbian from the age of 14 to 25, April wrestled with her sexuality throughout three long-term relationships before deciding a change was crucial. She stumbled through trying to find the perfect woman, party life, alcohol abuse, depression, and suicide attempts. Through a spiritual process and journey with the Lord, she gave her life over to God. As a result, while serving in the Army in Iraq, she met the man who would become her husband and now has three beautiful children with him.

Now a retired LAPD police officer, April works with Changed Movement to bring awareness to the political arena that it is possible to escape the homosexual lifestyle. April also works with Living Waters Ministry as a spiritual mentor and has a passion to share the healing power of the Gospel of Good News—Jesus Christ. After 11 years of marriage, her primary endeavor in life is to now embody the Proverbs 31 woman in her home. April says, "The Creator of the universe formed me in my mother's womb, scripture tells me—I am not a mistake! Now that I'm walking the Creator's path, I see the beautiful purpose He had for me all along."

Kevin Whitt
Dallas, Texas
United States
Age 42
Former Homosexual, Drag Queen,
Transgender, and Prostitute

I grew up in a dysfunctional home with a very abusive father. As a child, I endured verbal, physical, and sexual abuse. In the first grade, everyone called me "gay" and "faggot" because I seemed more feminine than other boys. Words are powerful, and I believed those lies. I began having same-sex attraction at a young age, and by age 15 I came out and started dressing in drag. I was embraced and accepted into a community of people that I could relate to, and the attention and recognition of dressing in drag became addictive.

As soon as I was old enough, I got into the club scene as an entertainer. Desperate for money, I started working in the adult industry as a transsexual prostitute, phone sex operator, dominatrix, and webcam "model." I thought this would be temporary, but earning over $1k a day became addictive, and I couldn't stop. Men made me feel sexy and wanted.

I hated Christians because all I'd ever been taught by the church was that gay people were going to hell and their punishment from God was to contract AIDS and die. So, I figured if I'm going to hell, I might as well have fun doing it. Eventually, I realized how toxic and addictive my lifestyle had become. Many friends and acquaintances had died young from HIV, and I saw others ruin their lives with drug and alcohol addictions.

One day while working in a male strip club, one of the stripper boys invited me to go to church. I thought it was weird, but I was open to it and went. That day, a seed was planted in my heart.

A few months later, I got invited to church on Easter Sunday. God grabbed my attention through a modern-day version of the resurrection of Christ being played out on stage, and I began to cry. I saw all that Jesus had done for me. That was the first day of my walk with Christ.

Eventually, my desires to do drag, party, or have sex lessened. God began speaking to me, and I got rid of all of my female clothing and accessories. My heart began to change dramatically as God continued to show me my true identity. I did not come to Christ seeking change in my sexuality. I simply came to Him with the desire for a healthy life and kept an open mind and loving heart. He did the rest.

I now understand that my sensitivity and interests in art, fashion, and beauty do not equate to homosexuality. American culture places a stigma on men. If we don't watch football and act a certain way, we must be gay. But that is a lie. I am created in God's image, and He gave me a creative mind. I love being a man just the way I was designed to be.

I was born with a rare heart defect called Transposition of the Greater Vessels, which means the heart is reversed. In 1978 when I was born, they had just begun doing the corrective surgery, so all of my nurses and doctors have always called me a "miracle baby." In my crazy life as a transsexual, I was spared from contracting HIV, even after sleeping with several people who were positive.

Later in life, I was diagnosed with multiple sclerosis, a crippling autoimmune disease. But even after all of that, I am still alive. I think I was created for such a time as this in order to use my testimony of change to influence our government to change their minds on the indoctrination of children by LGBTQ activists and the liberal agenda.

It is so evident I am not a mistake!

Alessio Lizzio
Italy
Age 33
Former Homosexual
Ministry–AmorePuro
Ministero Ex-LGBT
www.facebook.com/
amorepurogesu
www.amorepurogesu.com
info@amorepurogesu.com

I was born in Sicily, Italy. Some decades ago, homosexuals were seen very badly here in Sicily. However, with time, things have changed. When I came out to my parents, it was a dramatic experience. My mother burst into tears, and my father even fainted.

There were a few weeks of "grieving" at home, but after a while, the tears dried up. My boyfriend at the time was eating and sleeping at our place. I was never able to open up and talk with my parents beyond superficial things; I always felt a sense of shame, as if my opinion and emotions didn't matter in the end. All the while, homosexual desires were growing little by little, yet my self-esteem was shrinking.

From childhood, I experienced women squashing and domineering men. I had certain female teachers telling me I was not as good as the others, and I was being teased by my classmates, mainly girls. The final straw was being rejected by the only (and last) girl that I really liked, so I gave in to the attractions I was feeling toward men.

I was searching for the characteristics in men that I was lacking (or at least felt I was lacking), such as enterprising, resourceful, masculine, self-confident, etc. I chased after men because I wanted to possess their masculinity, but it only worked for a short while. After having sex, the emptiness was there all the same, and so it was for 10 years. I felt dirty. I felt I had betrayed myself and my father. I began to wonder why sex between two men was so perverse ...

One day my cousin invited me to church. At this point I was an atheist, yet I asked God to free me from homosexuality. I cried that day, but nothing really changed. A friend then suggested that I attend a pro-gay church where I could "accept myself" and they could "love me" as I was. By this point, I had read the Bible and understood that homosexuality was not pleasing to God, but I was unable to imagine myself being free from this identity.

For me, these homosexual desires were who I was, so I wondered, "Why would God make me like this if He wants to save me?" I attended this church community for three years, and I became a type of promoter of gay theology, but I was not changed. I had only made a "god" in my own image and likeness. In 2013, I attempted suicide. I was doing whatever I wanted, the world was accepting me and telling me that I was born gay, but I was not happy. Deep down, I knew it to be a lie. When I was younger, I liked girls, but the more I grew, the more the hurt inside of me intensified—the hurt from an inferiority complex, insecurity, and not feeling loved.

One day on the bus, I heard the voice of God tell me, "Search on YouTube for 'healed from homosexuality'." So I did. I found a testimony of an American ex-gay pastor. I saw a bit of myself in his story. I began to cry there on the bus while God said to me, "See? I didn't create you gay. There is a wound in your heart that the devil got into, and you believed him."

It was the most beautiful day of my life. I arrived home, kneeled down, and asked God for forgiveness for all my sins.

I believed that His Son Jesus died for me on the cross and resurrected from the dead. That very day, I received the Holy Spirit, and homosexuality and the gay lifestyle are now only a bad memory of the past. Today, does it still happen that I am tempted? Yes, but homosexuality and I are not one and the same thing because now I am one with Jesus—"For if we have become united with Him in the likeness of His death, certainly we shall also be in the likeness of His resurrection" (Romans 6:5).

For seven years now, I have been serving the Lord in street evangelism with the poor and in an ex-gay ministry. Jesus has given me peace, joy, and eternal life and has restored my true identity as a man and son of God. I know that I am not a mistake or an accident. God has created us for His glory and has saved us to bring us Home.

Richard Thomas
Laguna Beach, California
United States
Age 65
Former Homosexual
AIDS / HIV+ for over 42
years

June 26, 2021

Before I share my story and my testimony, I would like to share with you how the Lord brought me and Jim Domen together. It was when I was coming out of the homosexual lifestyle. It was back in 2000 when we met at the Vineyard Church in Anaheim. We were two broken men without a clue of what we were doing, but the Lord did. This was how we began our journey with Jesus.

I can't believe how Jesus uses broken men like us to wake up the wise and how it started from the beginning, knowing who we really are. I was such a broken man as I came into this world, not knowing how broken I was!

As a child growing up, I knew I was a little different, but I didn't know why. As we walk into this lifestyle as I did without knowing the truth, we realize we're walking into darkness.

When you're young and living the gay lifestyle, it can be fun for a season. But as you get older, it's like quicksand. It's hard to get out. But there is a way out, and His name is Jesus. The gay community desperately needs Jesus. They need to know that there is a way out of their confusion, shame, and misery. They need to know that if they die in their sin, they will go to hell. They need to know the truth. They need to know that God loves them and wants to save them and deliver them and heal them.

They need to hear the good news of the Gospel of Jesus Christ! I know it's hard, but we have to learn how to overcome our sin nature by taking the time to read and study the Bible. Everything we need to know will be shown to us through God's Word, which is one of the greatest gifts of all.

I love what a fellow believer told me years ago: the word "Bible" stands for **B**asic, **I**nstruction **B**efore **L**eaving **E**arth, so take the time to read the Bible. As we grow in God's Word and follow His will for our lives, we will go through trials and tribulations—and that's not easy!

Indeed, I did walk in darkness, not knowing where my life would go, but Jesus did as God's Word says in Romans 12:2, "And do not be conformed to this world but be transformed by the renewal of your mind that you may prove what is that good acceptable and perfect will of God."

Remember at the time I didn't understand what this really meant, but this is where He was cleansing me and showing me the truth through His Word. The deeper I went into the lifestyle, it nearly killed me. I became HIV positive in 1980, and what a journey it's been. But the Lord's been faithful and keeping me alive to share my testimony to the world and what that lifestyle will do to you. That's why God wrote the book of Proverbs, so the world would have instructions for knowing how to live.

It's been 21 years now since I've been walking with Jesus, and what a time it has been. It's not easy when you've been broken your whole life and don't know anything. But as we study through God's Word, He'll show you what you should've done.

I'm a witness of faith in learning what Jesus can do and how to walk in the Spirit and not in the flesh. As we go out into the world, I see things that I didn't see until God showed me the truth and gave me wisdom of what not to do.

We all want to be loved, but we have to learn the difference between lust and love. The flesh is like imagination in the way we think. Many will disagree with me and what I'm saying, but for now, it's your way of life. But there will come a time when you will put it all together, and it will be very damaging to you. It's very hard to change back because I know it too well.

Just think about it. Don't let your mind think for you. It's a choice how we live. We never think of that until it's too late. This is just the facts of life. We think nothing's going to happen, but it will in time. I wish sometimes I could go back and change something when I didn't know it was wrong at the time.

We have to keep learning and sharing our pain with others. Our journey in life can be a challenge or difficult or we have to make mistakes to learn from them. It is even shameful to learn all of our evil ways that we do to ourselves.

As I look back over the years, I see how God was so faithful in bringing good men into my life and showing me the love of Jesus. In the book of Proverbs, chapter 20, verse 5, it says, "Counsel in the heart of a man is like deep water, but a man of understanding will draw it out." So, there you go—God's Word is still alive because that's what happened to me! And what I am realizing is that the Lord is in control of our lives. He wants to bless us in who we are in Christ, and He's so faithful in providing.

So, whoever reads this, I hope you take a leap of faith and just ask God to help you to see the truth. God bless you!

thomasrichard270@gmail.com

Jake Mchaffie
Anaheim, California
United States
Age 32
Celibate Who Deals with
Same-Sex Attraction

Before Jesus, I didn't know who I was. My identity was flimsy as it was based on my athletic and academic performance, and the only reason I didn't implode before Christ was that my performances were good enough to make my family proud. But I was on really shaky ground. I grew up in a very normal, functional, and comfortable suburban family with both parents and a younger brother and a handful of neighborhood kids to hang out with. I was very shy as a kid and would often do more observing than talking. I was a keen student of every subject and a hard worker. I gave my parents hardly any trouble, and I was the ideal child by middle class suburbia standards.

I started to notice my attraction to guys around the 10th grade, but for some reason, I just didn't stress about it and figured it was probably a phase. I had the professional goal of becoming a veterinarian, and I had big athletic goals as well, being a varsity cross country and track athlete. These goals sort of took priority for the rest of high school over pursuing a relationship, even though I did go to a handful of high school dances with girls. I didn't necessarily feel like I was faking anything because I just was never one of those people who obsessed about putting a sexuality label on myself to begin with.

I didn't necessarily think of myself as gay or bisexual because I just thought that all teenagers experienced various attractions as they went through puberty. I knew what these identity labels were but just never felt in a rush to adopt one of them for myself, even though I knew I was different. I still feel like I thought certain girls were good looking, and I still remember feeling nervous about asking them to dances. I honestly don't know whether I felt a genuine attraction or not.

My eyes would notice guys' bodies a little too much, almost involuntarily, and I would try to avert my gaze to avoid notice. I would have never dared shower in the locker room at school for fear of getting an accidental erection that would ruin my reputation for the rest of high school.

I still don't know if I'd really met Jesus, but in my sophomore year of college at UC Davis in autumn of 2008 during probably the loneliest season of my life, a new friend I had just met suggested I check out Discovery Christian Church. It was there under the teaching of a brilliant pastor who happened to have a PhD in marine biology to boot that I ended up finally understanding the reality of my sin and my need for a Savior and made the decision to follow Christ.

I honestly can't tell you when the moment was that I made my decision. All I know is the Word of God just resonated as the truest thing I had ever read and heard, and I just couldn't help but be drawn to it.

In 2014 at age 25, I ended up finally accepting the reality that my attraction to men did not seem to be a phase and that it was the predominant attraction I found myself experiencing as an adult. I reached what could have been my crisis of faith moment/season in the fall of 2014 in my third year of grad school when I acknowledged this before the Lord and confessed that I didn't know how I was going to do this for another few decades. I promised Him that even if He didn't take this same-sex attraction away, my life would be His. And if He would truly never leave me nor forsake me like He promised, then I'd be okay.

Over the past half-dozen years, I've really grown satisfied in being single for the Lord, although I'm still working on the undivided devotion part that 1 Corinthians 7:35 mentions. I've really enjoyed getting to minister to all types of hurting people with my time, talent, and treasure. I've also had some incredible moments of cooperation with the Holy Spirit, leading up to these ministry activities that I wouldn't trade for even five minutes of a same-sex relationship.

One of the most pervasive lies Satan has spoken over my generation is that a pattern of temptation is the equivalent of an identity. I really hope to be able to be a resource empowered by the Holy Spirit to equip more Millennials and Gen-Zers to confront this lie and trust in Christ for their salvation, their sanctification, and their satisfaction, moment by moment and for eternity.

I'm not a mistake because my body is a temple of the Holy Spirit and comes from God, and I have been bought with an eternally valuable price, the blood of Christ, which makes me an heir of the kingdom of heaven and a son of the Most High.

Angel Colon
Orlando, Florida
United States
Age 31
Former Homosexual
Pulse Night Club Massacre
Survivor (after being shot
seven times)
Ministry–Co-Founder
of Fearless Identity,
FearlessIdentity.co

My life before I pursued change in my sexuality was what I would call "A Hot Mess." Lonely, empty, unhappy, shackled, and unloved was how I felt for eight years. The more unhappy I was, the worse it got. My life was so consumed by homosexuality, drugs, and liquor that I wouldn't give the time of day to my family. Having been raised in a strong Christian home, I felt a deep conflict between what I had known to be good and right and the life I was living. Even being in the lifestyle, the Holy Spirit would always tug at my heart. I would have moments when I would weep while talking to Jesus and moments when I would be drunk in the club or party and start singing worship songs. Even living in the lifestyle, I always knew the Lord was calling out my name. I ignored those calls until the year 2016, when I was fed up with my life. I had what I wanted and who I wanted but no happiness, real love, or peace.

One morning, I woke up hungover after a night of drinking and drug use, and later that evening, I ended up at Pulse Gay Night Club in Orlando with some friends. 2:02 a.m. is when everything changed. Saying our goodbyes, we heard a big POP!

I dropped my drink, realizing the sounds were gunshots. As we ran, I was shot several times. I fell down pulling my friends with me. As I was struggling to stand back up, I felt a foot step on the back my left leg and heard a loud snap which resulted in my left femur being broken. I couldn't move or even feel my legs, so I covered my head and stayed still.

What followed was chaos all around me. I started comforting the lady lying next to me, whispering to her to pretend to be dead. I looked at her and then heard a loud shot. As her eyes shut, I couldn't believe I had just witnessed her death. I was terrified I was next. Feeling the shooter behind me, I uttered what I thought would be my last prayer. Even in that terrible moment, the peace and hope of God flooded me. I heard a loud shot and felt my body jump up and down as I was being shot again. I thought I was dead. After several minutes, I started hearing cop radios. I raised my hands and called out, "Please come get me! I'm alive!"

As I recovered mentally, physically, and spiritually, I caught myself fighting with the Lord about my temptations through my process. One night, I fell on my knees and surrendered. In my prayer, I said, "Lord, I surrender. Take my struggles and temptations, but not only that, take my whole heart. Take everything of me!" And at that moment, the Holy Spirit spoke to me and said, "Angel, that is all He wanted. He wanted all of you, not just bits and pieces."

At that moment, I realized I was focusing on my sin instead of focusing on the person who was in charge of transforming my life—Jesus. I prayed day and night to be straight when all along I needed my whole heart to be restored. I needed to focus on my relationship with Jesus and getting to know Jesus because He is the Truth and the Truth shall set you free. That is how I was able to find true freedom and true identity. I can now wake up every morning and say, "I AM GOOD WITH GOD!"

My life today is a complete 180 from the life I had before. Feeling empty and lonely inside was slowly destroying me, but I now know what was needed to be fulfilled in my life—a true relationship with Jesus. I was able find out what true freedom was, and now the Lord has permitted me to be one of the co-founders of Fearless Identity with ministry partner Luis Ruiz as we share our stories with the world of what the Lord has done in our lives and help equip the body of Christ in how to welcome the LGBTQ community with open arms because the harvest is coming back to Jesus Christ.

Now that I'm living in the Lord, I know that I am not a mistake and that everything that has happened in my process is all in His will. Not only has my life changed completely, but because of that change, I have been able to join others in their journeys of finding freedom, finding their identity in Christ, and finding true peace, happiness, and love.

Luis Javier Ruiz
Orlando, Florida
United States
Age 38
Former Homosexual
Pulse Night Club Massacre
Survivor (Trampled after
helping people escape)
Ministry–Co-Founder
of Fearless Identity,
FearlessIdenity.co

I remember when Lady Gaga's song "I Was Born This Way" sounded so loud and real because I had same-sex attraction ever since I can recall.

My mother and father were present. I am so thankful they raised me the best way they knew how and asked God for the blueprint and manual on raising a son and daughter. It would be "on-the-job training," learn as you go. My father was in the military, so unfortunately, he had to leave for training quite a bit. This left me to pick up mannerisms, emotions, and feelings that led more to a feminine side than masculine. I was exposed to pornography and sex from a friend of the family's older son at a young age.

See, my father was present and loved me the best way he could. When a father doesn't show an emotional tie with his son, another man will, so sexuality was introduced by an abuser rather than talked about in a family setting where I could expose the abuse without shame or guilt. I found out later in life that our disconnection was due to an abuser in his life as a child. Living in shame and guilt with that secret, he was almost afraid to get close to me emotionally because of it.

When I was about 10 years old, my parents came to know Jesus from parties, and a life outside the church changed our lives forever. I remember as a kid hearing different types of preachers speak poorly about the homosexual community about how every other sin is redeemable by God, but homosexuality was the ultimate sin for some reason. It caused me to learn how to hide and deceive my parents and friends at an early age—living afraid that anyone would find out.

I remember a lesbian friend being the popular girl in high school, and words like "fag," "queer," and "gaylord" were fuel for her activism and then mine. Later on, I joined the military and proved to my dad that gays could make it in the Army. A life without Jesus led me to drunken nights. It led me to wake up in all kinds of beds, not knowing the person. It led me to try drugs and live a very sexually promiscuous life.

Listen, I was a HOE. I was having so much fun, but what's fun if there is no joy? I self-medicated, trying to fill a void by sleeping in California king-sized beds with my partners but a million miles away in my head. There was something inside of me crying out, "You were made for more."

Everything for me was hyper-sexualized. I was the life of the party, the military Puerto Rican Latin boy invited to all the five-star parties and dancing with my shirt off and sleeping with men, especially married military men in the closet. Every relationship I was in became tainted by cheating. Today, you are the top model, and tomorrow, the next top model will replace you.

During one drunk night of dinging around, I ended up in front of a church. Out of all places, a church—the place I had been running from for years. A place where they wanted me to "pray the gay away," whatever that means. They wanted me to get married because that's what salvation looked like more than living out the fruits of the Spirit. I was in front of a church where I gave my life to the Lord that night and was in deep for a whole year, getting Bible knowledge and reading it to become a better debater instead of allowing it to change my life and grow into the image of Jesus.

I remember men talking about their porn issues and the things they did with women and raising my hand. As soon as I said I like men, there were crickets. These men who hugged me tight and kissed me on the forehead now shook my hand from a distance, saying they were praying for me. This distance caused me to keep my struggles secret, learning how to fight it on my own. It was a trap sent from the devil to see me fall. He knew the more I struggled alone, the heavier life in church would become, and it did. We can't do this alone.

I remember two friends of mine at the Orlando Millenia Mall inviting me to Pulse Night Club. I had disconnected from everyone for a year, so there was an internal war inside me fighting to go. See, I didn't have to fight and struggle alone, but the lies I believed stopped me from talking to leaders and pastors because I thought they would not understand. It was all a lie because all the enemy wanted was to get me alone like a gazelle away from the herd so he could come at me like a lion to trap me. I fell for it.

On my birthday weekend, I wanted to be around people who I thought understood me. Later on, I came to find out those same people would turn their backs on me when I chose Jesus and lived out the whole truth of God's Word and not bits and pieces to fit my lifestyle. I remember going to a house party where I saw another Pulse survivor and good friend of mine, Angel Colon. It was the last time I would see him before his life was transformed from the shooting. He asked me, "Luis, are you going to Pulse?" I said, "Absolutely, I'll see you there."

It took everyone almost 45 minutes to decide to go, and not everyone came back. Two females who wanted us to stay at the party did not come back. We had lots of food and alcohol. We finally got to Pulse Night Club not knowing that all our lives were about to change. It was the last call for alcohol. Everyone was closing their tabs, and some were still having fun dancing. I remember hearing sounds like fireworks, and looking at my friend, I said, "Wow, those fireworks sound so close." In Orlando, that's normal with all of the parks here, but it sounded like it was inside the club this time. I heard people yelling, "Run!" I looked over to my friend, and by the time the shooter was in front of us, it was only by the grace of God that I was not shot.

My friend and boyfriend were both shot, and then Angel Colon on the floor just steps in front of me was shot. I remember running out of the door with a crowd trying to get out of the small door. People lay on the floor everywhere, many of them screaming, and the shots were getting louder and louder. People were running into the bathrooms and trying to hide. The shooter, Omar Mateen, was locked and loaded. After running out through the patio door to the other side of the club, several of us were kicking through a fence and my foot got stuck in it. I fell to the ground. Everyone in a panic trying to survive trampled me, making it painful to get up.

I called my mom to say I loved them and that I was sorry. My mom heard the gunshots, tried to answer me, and then the phone died. *This is it,* I thought. I was about to die as the gunshots kept getting closer and closer. Some guy came inside to help. Eventually, I was sitting at a 7-Eleven, listening to gunshots going off. Later on, we found out that we had escaped again because there was a car with a bomb inside, ready to be blown up.

I remember being at the hospital a day later because I was in so much pain. I remembered the helicopters, the ambulance, and bodies on the floor. People being medevacked. People crying and looking for their friends who were nowhere to be found. It was a horrible night and how thankful I was to make it out alive. Locating and calling my friends as I saw names of the deceased come up on the screen little by little. Sitting back the whole day, glued to the TV. Not being able to sleep, feeling afraid.

Weeks later, I was diagnosed with HIV. I remember just breaking down in my room right after that, crying so hard and looking up, yelling in my room, "God, why?" I didn't understand what was happening and said, "I am a gay man. What do you want from me?"

I then felt the heavy presence of the Lord and heard Him say to my heart, "It's not a gay-to-straight thing. It's a lost-to-saved thing." Then and there, I surrendered all of my life to Him, including my sexuality. After giving my heart to Jesus, I knew the process was going to be a journey. I needed counseling and healing from brokenness and trauma. I needed a place where I could meet Christ and find the root issue of why I was sexually broken and needing to self-medicate for past issues that were never healed.

Today, I thank Jesus for the finished work on the cross and for His blood that washed my sins away. I know that I am not a mistake. He accepted me as I was but loved me too much to keep me where I was. Sharing my story with thousands and in different countries has been so healing. Seeing people giving their hearts to Jesus is the best part. What the enemy meant to kill, steal, and destroy, God has turned into good. He has turned my mess into a message, putting me in His story.

Aleksandra Leśnik
Poland
Age 27
Former Lesbian

It all started when I was a 7-year-old girl addicted to porn. It severely affected my mind, emotions, and sexuality. In fact, this addiction wrecked my personality.

A lack of healthy relationships with my parents only made things harder. My 20s were dramatic. I was a young woman suffering from bipolar disorder. I didn't have much hope left.

The most challenging period of my life was when I was still in my hometown, Grudziądz (Poland). It was during my graduation class when I was going to go to university that I experienced a most profound depression and dreadful suicidal thoughts. I was no stranger to this as these feelings had accompanied me since childhood. However, at this stage, they had become unbearable!

At the time, a wonderful and brave psychotherapist played a big role in my life. She used to say to me during our sessions, "I feel deep in my heart that you are not a lesbian. You are struggling with deep and complicated identity problems. I do not deny that you feel same-sex attraction, but I believe that one day you will be a happy wife and mother." I knew she was not judging me or trying to convince me of anything, and the compassion she had shown was simply undeniable. Thanks to this, the truth about me was sown like a fertile seed in the soil of my heart for two years, and after a while, it produced good fruit.

Since then, I also knew that same-sex attraction was the result of many factors from the past, including the lack of a father figure, fearing him, lack of a healthy relationship with my mother, a strong need to protect my mother, addiction to pornography, etc. It was one of the key moments because the therapist gave me hope that change was possible.

Even though both my family and society accepted me as a lesbian and were supportive of my choices, deep inside I was unhappy, realizing that I didn't want to live such a life. Hearing the Biblical truth about God's unconditional love for me was a massive turning point. I encountered the living Jesus Christ. I invited Him into my heart. I got saved and experienced the overwhelming love of God that changed me from the inside out through the power of the cross!

Through God's abundant grace I found help, support, and love at church. Not only did I receive pastoral support at Church of Glory in Warsaw (Poland), but my sexuality was also transformed. I have experienced supernatural healing and a lot of miracles in my new life. I started a journey of growing and maturing in faith and became a singer and worshipper, promoting biblical and ethical values.

Today, I am free from unwanted same-sex attraction. I'm living a life of victory in my Savior Jesus Christ. I am passionate about reaching out to the local communities and beyond, educating others regarding homosexuality and sharing the simple Gospel message. As a heterosexual woman, I look forward to getting married and having children!

Why I am not a mistake? Because God created me in His image, He loves me, and He destined me for an amazing life and journey with Him which can help or inspire others and has a meaning for the world. Each of us is precious to God! So, nobody is a mistake! :)

Christopher
California
United States
Age 27
Former Homosexual

I "came out" after years of silently struggling with same-sex attraction. I thought I would finally be happy, but I rapidly began turning into someone I did not know. My friends celebrated me as I grew more flamboyant, and I basically put on a show for them.

I experienced God's love in a very powerful way while walking home through a forest. I found out that He loves me so much. His love was great enough to break my 11-year pornography addiction and give me the courage to follow Him. Most of my friends deserted me over time.

I've not looked back once since that day in the forest. I've forgiven every abuser, allowed God to heal this heart of mine, and dedicated my life to serving Jesus Christ.

I am not a mistake. I never was. God created me and every other person for a purpose on this earth. No one is a mistake. He loves us on purpose.

Edward Byrd
Age 34
Washington, D.C.
United States
Former Transgender/
Gender Fluid Androgenous
Known As "Remi"

I used to be known by the name of "Remi," a female persona I used to mask the dysfunction and pain of my past. During this season of my life, I pursued sex, drugs, and rock 'n roll. Finding it difficult to understand my pain, I turned to stripping and found myself involved in exotic sexual activities to find worth and value within myself. I was consumed with the culture and lifestyle of homosexuality; I became convinced it was my only identity.

However, I began to face severe depression and felt disjointed about life. I had faced so many disappointments as well as broken and abusive relationships. Recognizing the destructive cycles I continually found myself in, I started to ask questions. Could this be all there is to life? Will I ever experience a truly fulfilling life? I needed answers or else I was headed toward ending my life.

Feeling desperate, I searched for other stories like mine on YouTube. Finding videos of people who sought help to find freedom for themselves led me to pursue counseling, support groups, and online teachings. Some key social groups supported my efforts to leave that life that had led to further pain and destruction. Through these resources, I learned I had built my life on so many fabrications, and I had to deconstruct the false realities to discover my true identity.

My life today is absolutely nothing like before. I am a whole new person inside and out. I now I have incredible purpose, joy, love, acceptance, and peace in my life. Nothing in my past compares to the truth and love I have received from Christ and from the people in my life. I no longer look for fulfillment in dangerous places; I am fulfilled and secure in my sexual identity as a man—I am not a mistake!

James C Parker
Australia
Age 53
Former Homosexual and
Gay Activist

I had always believed I was born gay. I came out at 17 and was affirmed in my gay identity by family and friends.

At 18, I moved from the country to a city university and was the first person ever to come out publicly. I was affectionately known as the "college queer," and I threw myself into gay activism. I'd been raised in a Christian home and continued to pray, so I joined the city's Lesbian and Gay Christian Group.

At first, I was promiscuous, but then I met my "Mr. Right." He was ex-military and ticked all my boxes. We were polar opposites as I was effeminate, yet we remained monogamous throughout our relationship.

A year or so after starting to date, a solid Christian guy at university approached me and invited me to a Christian gathering of young people. I agreed to attend, and the passion with which the young people worshipped God was palpable. I became healthily envious of their ability to actually "know" Him. I knew a lot about God but had no personal relationship with Him. This soon changed.

I suddenly heard the Gospel message of "repent and believe." I responded by saying sorry to God for whatever might stand in the way of me receiving His love. I asked Him to forgive me and to send me His Holy Spirit. I learned to pray, and within weeks, my boyfriend noticed such positive changes in me that he too committed his life to Christ. We were soon hailed as the model gay Christian couple. Life couldn't get better, or so I believed.

My prayer life accelerated beyond my boyfriend's, such that I began to feel an increasing unease with our model relationship. I began to feel challenged between my lover and Christ. Nothing and no one had touched my heart like Jesus. After much inner stirring, I chose Christ as my primary lover. As I exchanged the worldly label of "gay" for my true identity in Christ, what transpired shocked me to the core.

Through deep prayer and the insightful work of a Godly therapist, I came face to face with crippling inner wounds I had never previously seen—traumas from being abandoned at birth and adopted, years of childhood sexual abuse and exposure to pornography, and an innate distrust of men and of women.

I learned to repent, forgive, ask for forgiveness, reject my thoughts, and take on God's mind. I precariously learned to trust men and women. Slowly, the true man hidden deep within me began to rise.

As my heart focused on deeply engaging with other men, my erotic preoccupation with everything masculine lessened. From there, I yearned to search for a new "mystery," discovering this in women. Some years later, I ended up marrying a wonderful lady and becoming a father.

The growing peace and dignity I am discovering through Christ is beyond words. Wouldn't I be selfish and foolish not to want others to experience this same love and inner freedom?

I'm not a mistake because, although having been conceived within a 3-week love affair, I have learned that my old birth came from mortal sperm, but my new birth came from God's living Word. (The Bible, 1 Peter 1:23)

Jeremy Luke Bate
Australia
Age 55
Former Transgender
Who Transitioned and
De-Transitioned

At age five, I was experiencing gender confusion. I was learning to read, and I associated the female characters with myself despite knowing I was a boy. It was a confusing and shameful experience. These feelings continued for years, some times more prevalent than other times, like an addiction that never went away. I never told anyone.

Eventually, after bringing up two children with my partner of nine years and having ongoing inner gender conflict, I read in a book the definition of "transsexual" and thought this applied to me. When the relationship ended in my early 30s, I sought treatment, going to a doctor and getting referred to a psychiatrist.

The psychiatrist had previously treated two transsexuals who committed suicide after "affirming treatment," so he was reluctant to do the same with me. After several weeks of frustration, I realized he wouldn't prescribe the hormones I desired, so I saw another psychiatrist who, after a brief history intake, gave me a prescription for estrogen and referred me to an endocrinologist.

I transitioned and became who I thought was the real me, and my family was reasonably accepting. I had a new female partner who supported me during the process, culminating with sex-reassignment surgery in 2003. I was only required to see the Melbourne gender team's psychiatrist once and had a single one-hour session with a psychologist. I told the psychologist that I didn't want to go against nature, and her reply was, "What about going against your own nature?"

On the morning of my operation in the Melbourne hospital, I had doubts forming. I needed time to consider the implications that were confronting me in the stark reality of the moment, but I was rushed into surgery as if it was a tactic to prevent people from backing out. Another recipient of surgery I talked to during my hospital stay had a similar experience.

Once surgery was done, I continued life as a "transwoman," playing female soccer, studying, and working. Years later, my second long-term relationship ended after nine years, and I started an intensive period of inner work and spiritual study amidst extreme highs and lows of severe depression, which I saw as a spiritual crisis and refused numerous attempts by doctors to administer anti-depressants.

After years of this, I started a period of political awakening after being leftist and Communist for most of my life. I came to understand the globalist/cultural Marxist forces at work engineering society, and I found my new patriotic worldview put an end to my prolonged depression virtually overnight. I no longer needed to be concerned with my petty issues when there was civilization-level dramas to focus on. I questioned mainstream science, finding it was often based on dubious unquestioned assumptions and followed ideological agendas.

After this, I got an autism spectrum diagnosis which helped make sense of my life for the first time ever, dispelling years of confusion about many confounding aspects of my life and behavior.

Eventually, I looked into transgender medicine which I was avoiding because it was too close to home. I quickly discovered that the science was dubious with small samples, poor peer reviewing, biased assumptions, and mostly "light and fluffy" studies. I saw evidence that the medical field had been maneuvered into accepting "affirming treatment" by trans pressure groups within the professional bodies.

I started to consider detransitioning so was discussing the matter on a trans health Facebook group. I was immediately blocked, but not before finding out about DES (diethylstilbestrol), the anti-miscarriage drug given to millions of expectant mothers between the 1940s and 1970s. I realized my mother had taken it when pregnant with me. It is a potent estrogen that is known to cause gender identity issues in 20% of boys. The drug was continued for a generation after it was discovered to be ineffective and was only stopped when it was positively identified as the cause of a rare cancer cluster. This made me want to detransition even more.

I saw an endocrinologist and started taking testosterone, which had a beneficial effect. In fact, I had never felt like that before which led me to believe I was always low in testosterone, no doubt a consequence of the DES. The endocrinologist was in denial about my detransition, assuming I was becoming "non-binary." I found this was a common experience for detransitioners—clinicians refusing to believe or acknowledge the validity of detransition. It became clear that gender ideologists are reluctant to acknowledge detransition because it undermines the supposed need for affirming treatment. A frequent argument from transgender activists is that detransitioners could not have been real trans in the first place. The proof of this is that they detransitioned—something they claim a genuine trans person would never do.

After detransitioning, I questioned the "born that way" philosophy of trans and homosexuality and found it was the last of my misconceptions and prejudices that was preventing me from returning to the church. A friend shared information about reparative therapy, showing that homosexuality can change through therapy. My parents had stopped going to church when I was 16, so I fell away, affected like the culture as a whole by the left's indoctrination in the media, popular culture, and the education system. Now without even intending to, three months after detransitioning, I found myself back in a Catholic church, asking God to welcome me back. I was immediately overcome with a wave of love and welcoming. I realized it was all real—Jesus, God, and the Holy Spirit.

I saw my conversion as the first in many miracles at work in my life. At the time, I was experiencing intense and prolonged back pain. Eventually, I asked a Catholic friend to pray with me over the phone for the relief of the pain that I could no longer bear. Within two minutes, the pain reduced to a fraction of the intensity and never returned.

I am a weak, frail sinner who needs every grace God bestows on me. I am beset by temptations and difficulties, and I love humanity, despise sin, and strive to be worthy to be a soldier for Christ in this spiritual battle we call the world. I am glad to be the man I was created to be after renouncing my disobedience. I am not a mistake because God doesn't make mistakes.

Jesús Carbonell
Colombia
Age 51
Former Transgender

My name is Jesús Carbonell, and I am Colombian (South America). I was born in a dysfunctional family where emotional violence and physical aggression were normal. I grew up in an environment without values and limits, an extremely dangerous place for a child. I was six years old when I had the first of many sexual abuses that lasted for the following years, performed by men close to the family. Without understanding my emotions, I distorted the healthy model of love in the absence of meaningful relationships. I did not experience the unconditional love that every child needs, so I began to mentally distort and sexualize my affections without knowing.

I started a homosexual lifestyle at the age of 17 and then took a turn toward transgenderism. At 37, I was on my way to becoming a transgender woman and attending support groups for the definitive change of sex. Time passed, and I was happy with the changes, but my identity did not fit within the concept of the woman I thought I was.

However, as time went by, I was walking toward my own emotional descent, and I began to experience depressive crises to the point of wishing I was dead. My days were purposeless, and I was not finding my true inner fulfillment. My relationships with same-sex couples only gave me fleeting moments. That's why I thought the gender transformation would bring fulfillment to my being. What a great deception—all my effort was in vain.

While in the process of transformation, I became mortally ill and was diagnosed with various diseases. The medical prognoses gave me no hope. I was very hurt in my emotions, and that made me very angry with God because I asked Him many times to transform my world of lust, alcohol, and addictions, but I thought He was not listening to me.

In the year 2010, God's perfect plan came with His divine intervention to make me His. My transformation was radical. His power lifted me from the bed of death, healed me, and restored me from all my wounds. By then, I was living in Madison, Wisconsin, and at the invitation of a friend, I decided to go to his church. I was so sick that I couldn't walk, but at the end of the service, I went to the altar and was anointed with oil. This was the beginning of my holistic healing. I began to see myself with the real identity of God as He created me. I began to experience His love like never before, and His Holy Spirit has been transforming me. JESUS CHRIST is the most powerful experience I have ever had!

One day, I had a vision in which I was following Christ in the middle of a storm in the desert. Behind me, a long line of families followed me. Then I understood His call to bring healing to those who believe that homosexuality can be transformed. There are extreme positions that condemn this condition completely, bringing judgment and condemnation. On the contrary, the Ministry Transformed by Jesus Christ (which I lead) clings to the truths of freedom from sexual addictions. We offer loving and unconditional support to those struggling with same-sex attraction, educating family members, friends, pastors, and the church at large.

Through the Beyond Hope Restoration Program, we help raise awareness through the education of emotions and spiritual freedom, edifying the body of Christ to walk in freedom from sexual brokenness, addictions, and drugs through establishing a personal relationship with Jesus Christ and the healing power of the Holy Spirit.

Karen Lee
Singapore
Age 44
Former Lesbian

Even though my parents' marriage was failing, I still received love and attention from my Grandma. My grandma was the one I loved most with memories of toys, candies, and fun.

That year, Mom turned into both gambler and chain-smoker and abandoned me and my sister. She was emotionally unstable, leaving Dad as the breadwinner who worked hard and tried to give us comfort. Yet, Mom left during my formative years when I needed her the most.

Psychologists say that what happens to children in their early years has a long-term effect on them. I can remember sketchy details of a traumatic incident but it is not worth remembering. All I know is that it changed the life of a six-year-old forever.

I wasn't frightened when he first approached me. The tall man was Chinese, likely in his early 30s, with a thick moustache and very well dressed. He appeared to be friendly and claimed to be Dad's friend. He offered me a Chupa Chups, and I succumbed to the temptation, even though I was told not to accept candies from strangers. He led me to a deserted place and started running his hands through my hair, telling me how soft it was. He then gently rubbed my back and told me to lie down.

"Daddy never told me to do this," I said. I was confused, and had no idea what was going on.

"It's alright. I'm not going to hurt you, you little sweetie pie," he smiled, showing his decayed teeth.

His hands were then on my buttocks, gently squeezing them. I asked what he was doing, and again he flashed that sinister smile. I still remember those moth-eaten teeth and the smell of his raw breath.

Then he told me to stand up facing him. My emotions were mixed as I didn't understand what he was going to do to me. I became frightened and wished Mom were next to me. Tears started welling up in my eyes and heavy drops trickled down my rounded cheeks as I felt pain in my vagina. It was a short while before a passerby came by and scared him off. I ran as fast as my legs could take me into Grandma's arms.

The run seemed to take forever. Grandma came to the door. I leapt into her arms and cried bitterly. Till this day, the lie remains, "I was being chased by a fierce dog." The nightmarish incident haunted me for years.

That was the last time I wore a dress. I told myself I had to be strong. I needed to protect myself. I wanted to belong, feel loved, and be wanted. At 11, I thought it was just puppy love. At 13, I realized I was falling for female teachers and close female friends, and I longed to find out why. At 19, I flew to Sweden to have my first sexual rendezvous and became very promiscuous.

For five years, I sought to find answers, but internally, I was conflicted. At 24, I became one of the first five gay couples to get married. My Christian parents nearly disowned me, and I was so close to surrendering my Singaporean citizenship. Somehow, deep down, I was not at peace. I continued to live in a dysfunctional marriage which looked blissful on the outside. Three years into my marriage, I had multiple sexual relationships with other women which eventually ended our marriage of seven years.

I sought happiness in the wrong places, hoping I could find someone to fill my empty void but there was no one. I turned to pornography—gay men pornography. From that moment on, I was completely separated from the presence of God. This separation created a dryness in my soul, a devastating place to be. I was completely lost, and I felt death inside of me.

Then in 2018, I was driving home one afternoon when I felt God's undeniable presence in my car. I wept uncontrollably when I heard, "Come back to me, my child. Do not be a lesbian anymore." There was such gentleness and love in His voice that I knew it had to be God—not me and not the enemy for sure I thought.

After a week of struggle, I obeyed and repented. I walked away from living a homosexual lifestyle and chose holiness. Today, I am pursuing healing and restoration. I am lying if I tell you I no longer have same-sex attraction, but the same-sex attraction in me has significantly reduced because I do not seek it and I do not crave it.

I learned, "With man this is impossible, but with God all things are possible." I never knew I could turn my life around.

I also learned there is light at the end of those tunnels—the Light and Life of the world. Faith is not blind. On the contrary, it is by faith and trust that God is for me and not against me. I am running this race with perseverance and fixing my eyes on Jesus, the pioneer and perfecter of faith. I am definitely not a mistake.

Kathy Grace Duncan
Portland, Oregon
United States
Former Transgender (female to male then return to biological sex)

WALKING IN THE TRUTH

Growing up from as far back as I can remember, I felt I should have been a boy. All through school I would have crushes on girls, and I pretended to have girlfriends. I kept this as a secret the whole time. When I got older, I bought a car and started to live a double life—telling my parents one thing when in reality I was dating girls. After I graduated, I was desperate to live as a man. At the age of 19, I moved out, changed my name, and started taking male hormones. I thought I was so free. Life had finally begun for me, and I was excited to start living it as a man.

Two weeks after I started to live as a man, I met Jesus and accepted Him as my Lord and Savior. I didn't hear Him say anything about how I was living being wrong, nor did He strike me dead. So, I thought He was okay with how I was living.

I had a few girlfriends here and there, and I also got into a deep pornography addiction in the last relationship I was in. I had grown up in a dysfunctional family where my dad was abusive to my mom and my mom constantly the victim, and after being in this new relationship for a year, I realized she was my mom and I was my dad. Upon realizing this, I broke it off. I could not treat her like that, and I was not going to be that man.

After the breakup, I went back to church and got involved in the orchestra. One night on my way to orchestra practice, the Lord called to me and said, "Will you now? Will you now?" I took inventory and had nothing standing in the way so I said, "Yes, Lord, I will." That night after saying yes to the Lord, He delivered me from the porn addiction. I was leading a men's Bible study, involved with the junior high kids, in orchestra, and involved in the single's ministry.

It was four years after saying yes to the Lord when I was confronted by the church about who I was. I confessed I was a woman living as a man, and as I did, the Holy Spirit blew into me. I then knew I had to go back to being the woman He had created me to be. I started my journey after living as a man for 11 years.

It has been 28 years of being out of that lifestyle. The Lord has healed me greatly and deeply. I am content with living as woman, and I understand God has created me on purpose for a purpose. I have learned the importance of knowing who I am and how much I am loved. I don't long to go back to Egypt because this promise land flows with milk and honey.

Since I am no longer deceived about who I am, I clearly see I am no mistake and was created by an intentional God who loves me fiercely.

Rev. Tryphena Law
Malaysia
Age 51
Former Lesbian
Ministry–Pursuing Liberty
Under Christ, Malaysia

I was born into a Chinese family that practiced ancestral worship and believed filial piety was important. Being the eldest, my parents were expecting a boy and were probably disappointed that I was a girl. Nevertheless, within the next five years, they had four of us. My parents always reminded me to be a good role model for my siblings. I had the assumption that when I did good, I would be loved. I strove to be a good daughter, and yet I never felt that I measured up to their expectations.

As a child, I was dressed up like a boy and constantly played with boys' toys. My parents seldom affirmed my femininity but instead made jokes about my body size. I was on the bigger size and constantly being called "fat" or even "tomboy." Though I laughed along, deep within me, I was very hurt and ashamed of my body. I longed to be affirmed and loved.

When I was a teen, I was invited to my school's Christian Fellowship, and during one of the meetings, I felt the love of Christ overwhelm me. That day at the age of 13, I gave my life to Jesus, but it was also the same year that my angry father chased my mother and four of us out of the home after a heated argument. It was that day that my image of a man through my father was broken. I hated my father and vowed that I would never allow any men to bully us, and I vowed to do better than all the men in the world.

Even though I received Jesus, I never really had a relationship with Him. I continued to strive to please God through my good works. Though I hated my father, I did not want to see the family shattered, and I prayed that God would intervene. God did, and my parents reconciled, but my mother was hurt and could not trust my father. At the same time, I was never treated like a girl in school, and I felt so "ugly," both inside and outside. I began to numb my pain through porn. Each time after sinning, I ran to the Cross for forgiveness. But the cycle never stopped because I did not know where to look for help.

In my adulthood with a noble profession as a teacher and later after responding to God's call to be a full-time pastor, I continued to live a double life. It was when my partner left me for a man that I encountered God. I went to leave my house to commit suicide, but for more than an hour, I could not move. I wrestled with God, and He won. I did not die, but that day, I encountered God. He sent a community to journey with me. I left the ministry that day, but years later, God reinstated me back to serving Him and serving the LGBTQ who desire to be transformed by Christ.

Today, I am very certain that He did not make me a lesbian but rather His child. Even though I disobeyed Him, He has never taken away His image from me. I am created in His image, and He has given me a new identity—His beloved daughter. My past brokenness and pain and the painful path that I took will never define my future in Christ Jesus.

His beloved daughter,
Rev. Tryphena Law
Pursuing Liberty Under Christ, Malaysia

Sihol
Indonesia
Age 41
Former Homosexual

My name is Sihol, and I'm from Indonesia. I grew up in a nominal Christian family, and as a child, I was physically abused by my mom and had an emotionally absent father. I not only felt different because of the same-sex attraction, but I also hated my body. I didn't want to be perceived as effeminate, so I would be very careful with my gestures and voice.

It was exhausting. I felt like I was carrying a burden that I could only let go when I was alone in my room. I felt lonely. No one knew what I was going through. The self-hatred grew even more to the point that I tried to commit suicide. I really did try to change. I read the Bible so I knew that homosexual action is a sin. I couldn't reconcile my sexuality with my faith because I knew the truth. In the end, I decided to part with God. I thought if God couldn't or wouldn't change me and I'm going to hell, I might as well enjoy my way there.

I began to suppress the guilt and shame of my sinful life. In the end, I convinced myself that there is no God and I could do whatever I wanted to do as long as I didn't hurt anyone. But living this lifestyle didn't bring me the happiness that I thought it would. If anything, it was quite the opposite. It felt more like an endless search of pleasure, and the need simply kept getting bigger and bigger. I was never really satisfied until I had an encounter with God.

Three questions popped in my mind that day. *What have I become?* I realized I'd become a completely different person, and I didn't like this bitter person. *Is this lifestyle sustainable?* I realized that it's not sustainable. I couldn't keep doing what I was doing until old age, and even if I could, I didn't want to because it was just meaningless.

If there is no God, then what's the point of suffering? I realized there that if there is no God, then suffering is meaningless. And if suffering is meaningless, why not just kill ourselves? Then I realized there must be a God.

God started showing me my sins, but I didn't feel condemned. It was quite the opposite. God was inviting me to eternal life because my sins were destroying me. At first it was difficult because I'd already embraced the gay identity, but I took a leap a faith. I trusted the Lord. I knew there were many things I didn't understand, but I could trust Him. And so, I prayed and surrendered myself to Him, and that was just the beginning of my journey with Jesus.

Right now, I live a fulfilled and meaningful life. My search for love and fleeting pleasures has ended. I have found my rest in Christ Jesus. That doesn't mean I don't struggle or experience temptations. It just means I know that whatever comes, I have my refuge in the Lord, and I don't have to be anxious about life. I've also learned to love myself because if God loves me, why should I hate myself? He has created me fearfully and wonderfully but all for His glory, not mine. I only boast in the works of my Savior on the cross. I'm definitely not a mistake. Everything that has happened in my life, including my same-sex attraction, God used for His glory.

Wayne Chu
Taiwan
Age 40
Former Homosexual

CHANGED OR NOT CHANGED? IT'S ALL ABOUT MY UNIQUE CREATION.

Nobody taught me how to be a man or give recognition that I was doing good as a man. On the other hand, no one told me I was really gay or not. I just learned from the internet and what the society told me. This was me.

In my memory, many of my friends or classmates called me sissy. Most of the boys wouldn't accept me as one of them because I was so emotional and would cry so easily. Furthermore, they considered me as a girl because my body language was so feminine. Well, yes, I am very emotional and cry easily. I don't like to do sports because I hate to get sweaty. Because of that, if I can be a girl, maybe I could be happier? I could try.

I gave myself a girl's name when I was in second or third grade because that made me feel more comfortable. I tried to learn how a mother's life was, since she was the one who always took care of me emotionally and was willing to listen to my feelings. My father was so quiet and didn't know how to respond to anything, even now.

I kept asking my mother, "Why don't you give me another brother or sister? I feel so lonely." She couldn't because she had a rare blood type, and doctor told her it was too dangerous to have another child. How can a second-grade kid understand that? He can only get that he has to live like this his entire life.

There was a very good boy who was my best friend during my elementary school years. He was also an only child. We played together all of the time after school, and I felt so happy. But there was one thing he was down on me about that made me confused about my self-identity. One day, we were lying on the same bed when we felt tired. He put his hand put on my body and started to move it slowly to my private parts. I didn't resist but enjoyed it so much. After that, this kind of "game" became our normal interaction.

It began my fantasy with any masculine and good-looking man. I imagine that I can be hugged and stay in their arms, comfortable and beloved, especially when I was in puberty.

I know it's impossible to tell anyone about this because it's wired. Every time this type of man came near me, my heart-beat got stronger. I always tried to touch his body accidentally and allowed him to touch me and hug me for any reason. This made me struggle emotionally, and I didn't know who I could share it with. Was I only attracted by "men" at this confused period about love and sex? What's wrong with me? I didn't know why I couldn't respond when other male friends were sharing which types of girl were their favorite, how the girls' body were so good, etc. It made me feel so disgusting. "How can you guys describe girls like this? It's so mean," I'd say. On the other hand, I was so hungry to find someone who could share with about my favorite type man. And I found some other ways to release that desire—pornography and collecting men's pictures.

My mother's death when I was in 8th grade at the age of 14 was a bolt out of the blue to me. She was my pillar of every-thing. How could she just leave me, not telling me she had cancer? She was just gone like a flip of the finger without any notice. I couldn't cry because my culture told me if I cried, her spirit would stay in this world because of her worry. As a Chinese guy, I shouldn't cry because men only weep when deeply grieved. Did anyone understand my emotions and the need to release them? No one could but myself.

However, that was not the only pressure. My father was too weak to handle all of the things after my mother's death. I have to stand up and deal with it. I needed to be like a grown man and learn how to deal with the funeral, heritage, legal documents, insurance claims, etc. That was not the end. A year and a half later, my grandfather died. I had to handle everything again. I was totally collapsed.

I remember the day I was standing alone in my living room after finishing all the things. I couldn't stop and started to cry aloud. That was the first time I released my tears after my mother's death. I kept crying and crying. When I felt a little bit calm, I told to myself, *I'll no longer cry for anything. I hate being a man because men are useless. I want to be like my mother—a very strong, talented, brave woman."*

I wasn't doing good during my senior year in high school. It might have been because of my depression and hatred of my father. I decided to fly away to the other side of the Pacific Ocean, get rid of my family and my frustration, and try to start a brand-new life. It was here where Jesus found me again.

Why did I use the word "again"? Because I was student in a kindergarten that was part of the Episcopal Church. I remember I really loved going there and always prayed in the church building. After I went to elementary school, I stopped going.

There was the only one reason for me to go to church—feeling bored on the weekend. Life in North America is totally different than Taiwan. There is so much night life and entertainment in Taiwan, and public transportation is very convenient. However, in North America, you can't go anywhere easily if you don't have a car. Also, I can't believe that all of the stores close so early on the weekend. I don't know where I can go during the weekend. Those are the two reasons I decided to respond my friend's invitation to go to church.

The church brought me back to the warmness of home which is the biggest reason I decide to receive Jesus. After my mother and grandfather's deaths, I didn't know what "home" felt like, and God brought me back to the church. The second year after I joined the church, I decided to be baptized. This decision revealed a question that has confused me for a long time—should I identify myself as a gay?

After my baptism, I moved out of my dorm and started living with another brother. He was the one who got baptized at the same time I did. We were very good friends, and we could talk on the phone all night long. At the beginning of us moving in together, everything seemed normal. Then I realized one thing brought us into a temptation and caused us to fall all the way down—we decided to sleep on the same bed. One day after we watched a gay movie, we had our first intimacy interaction.

I have to say, before I received Jesus, my life can be described as "all right." The reason was simple—I didn't have any other choices. Before Jesus, I didn't even identify myself as a gay because I just didn't know. I freely visited gay porn websites, tried to boyfriends, collected as many as men's photos as I wanted, and have fantasies with any man. The most important point—I didn't need to consider my gay identification as a "problem."

I heard many messages from Sunday worship or theology teachings on "homosexuality is a sin." I received various responses after trying to share my gay issue with my pastors.

I experienced how churches reacted to same-sex marriage legalization. All these experiences made me feel very nervous because I just couldn't get rid of this so-called gay problem. I tried to read the Bible often. I tried fasting. I tried to receive healing and deliverance. I tried to forgive or ask for forgiveness for anyone or anything. I tried to control my desires and stop watching porn or handsome man pictures, but my feelings of attraction to men was still there.

No one in church could tell me what a "changed" gay looked like. The only evaluation was whether I was interested in marrying a woman or not. I just couldn't date a woman because I still felt like I was not a real man. I did try to date, but at the end, we broke up for the same reason—I didn't really understand what they wanted. It made me believe that I was totally gay and impossible to be changed. God had made me wrong, and He didn't love me. He hated me so much that He made me gay to have fun and torture me.

Rainbow 7 was a very special Christian organization that brought me a different theology perspective and helped me see differences in God's creation. That was the day I decided to give God one last chance. I told Him if I couldn't see any change this time, I would leave Him and choose my own life. I called Rainbow 7 and asked for help for the last time.

I can't remember everything that happened when I was in Rainbow 7's group, but I remember it was a very tough journey about my past, present, and even my future life. They helped me realize gay issues were not my biggest problem, and they also let me know that homosexual orientation is not the biggest sin in God's truth. There isn't any "biggest" sin in God's truth—sin is sin. There is no gray area in between.

The course started to help me review my belief system, inner world, and relationships with others, and also the theology I received. My inner eyes were getting clearer.

It turns out that all of this was only about my relationships and beliefs being implanted. Beliefs such as when I was young and someone gave me feedback that I wasn't suitable to be called a man, when my father couldn't give me enough affirmation that I'm a man, when I tried to learn how to be like my mother and she didn't teach me, when the church told me I had to change but couldn't clarify how the whole picture of Jesus' salvation and God's love of His creation worked. I was stuck in my limitation of human's knowledge and dualism. I couldn't see how God created a unique person like me as a tender, emotional, attentive man. Jesus accepted everything about me. Even when I kept falling down again and again, He was still willing to help me to stand up. The Holy Spirit gave me strength to face all of my dissatisfactions and the power to overcome them.

Gay is just a label for me right now. I don't need anyone to put any kind of label on me, such as gay, heterosexual, bisexual, changed, not changed, etc., because I understand "anyone is in Christ, he is a new creation." I believe I am unique and the one and only creation by God because "God created mankind in his own image." Any label is from humans because we all need some kind of definition for confirming our life is going the right way. But if we forget to focus on God's creation, any label will turn a person's life into a dead end alley, and they can't find a way out.

My son just had his first birthday, and my marriage with my wife is now into the third year. Being a father and a husband used to be impossible, but God gave me a miracle. I can't believe I can fall in love with a woman so deeply that we can have our child. Every time I look at my wife and son, I feel so happy and blessed. I know I can't achieve this, but God did everything.

I used to decide my life would end on my birthday when I turned 40. But at the time I wrote this story, it is three months after my 40th birthday. I remember on my 40th birthday, God told to me, "Wayne, today is your 40th birthday, and you used to decide today would be your last day in the world. And so, yes, today is really your last day in the world because after today, your life will be in my hand."

I used to identify as a gay, but I know gay can't describe the whole me. Now, I am who I am—I am God's unique and one-and-only creation. I don't need any label to define me because I am a whole man.

Kim Zember
San Diego, California
United States
Age 37
Former Lesbian
www.OvercomeMin.com

I started having desires for women in high school and began acting on them when I was 17. My desires for women, money, and comfort lead me down a path far from my Catholic upbringing. My lifestyle, coupled with the constant underlying fear of being alone, drove me to drown out the small whisper of God I would hear. Torn by my desires, I lived a double life, jumping back and forth from husband to girlfriends, drunken nights to morning church, Southern California real estate to nonprofit work in Ethiopia and being internally torn daily. I realized that I was in a vicious cycle of relationships that were not truly fulfilling. I felt deeply convinced that I needed to make big changes if I wanted different results in my life.

I became so desperate that I decided to surrender everything about the way I had been living and asked for Jesus to be Lord of my life and help me. From that moment on, the heaviness I had been living in for so many years began to lift. I made a personal commitment to myself to not date anyone until I gained clarity on who God had for me. I began to experience peace in my life, a peace that I had been searching for all along. I began to feel fulfilled in a way I had never. I felt like I was beginning to learn who I really was, my True identity.

When I chose to focus on Jesus and His love for me and growing in relationship with Him, I found myself free from anxiety, depression, and duplicity. I experienced living in an authenticity and freedom that I did not know was possible.

There is now no greater joy for me than sharing the love, freedom, and restoration I found through my personal relationship with Jesus Christ, whether in my hometown of San Diego or my 'home away from home', Ethiopia. For the first time in my life, I have found fulfillment in being 'single', with my eyes and heart set on Jesus and focused on the call He has on my life and the continued comfort and guidance from the Holy Spirit!

I know now that my life has purpose, because every day my Heavenly Father fills my heart with His love and then blesses me with the gift to go out and share His love with all those who do not yet know His love for them! To me there is no better purpose in life than to be loved by God and let others know of His perfect life changing love!

For more information on Kim's ministry for those experiencing same-sex attraction visit: www.OvercomeMin.com

Bibliography

[1] Gushee, D. P., McLaren, B. D., Tickle, P., & Vines, M. (2015). Changing our mind: a call from America's leading evangelical ethics scholar for full acceptance of LGBT Christians in the church. Read The Spirit Books, an imprint of David Crumm Media, LLC.

[2] https://www.pewresearch.org/social-trends/2013/06/13/a-survey-of-lgbt-americans/

[3] Maxwell, J. (2010). i.e., Everyone Communicates, Few Connect. Thomas Nelson Incorporated.

[4] Dallas, Joe. When Homosexuality Hits Home: What to Do When a Loved One Says, I'm Gay. Harvest House Publishers, 2015. Kindle edition. 69-71.

[5] McDonald, Greg, and McDonald, Lynn. Embracing the Journey: A Christian Parents' Blueprint to Loving Your LGBTQ Child. Howard Books, 2019. Kindle edition. 60.

[6] Dallas, Joe. When Homosexuality Hits Home: What to Do When a Loved One Says, I'm Gay. Harvest House Publishers, 2015. Kindle edition. 23.

[7] Sandort et al. "Same-sex Sexual Behavior and Psychiatric Disorders: Findings from the Netherlands Mental Health Survey and Incidence Study NEMESIS," Archives of General Psychiatry 58:85-91, 2001.

[8] Vroegop, Mark. Dark Clouds, Deep Mercy: Discovering the Grace of Lament. Crossway, 2019. Kindle edition. 26.

[9] Michel, Jen Pollock. Surprised by Paradox: The Promise of "And" in an Either-Or World. InterVarsity Press, 2019. Kindle edition. 155.

[10] Allberry, Sam. Is God anti-gay? (Questions Christians Ask). The Good Book Company, 2013. Kindle edition. 13.

[11] Dallas, Joe. When Homosexuality Hits Home: What to Do When a Loved One Says, I'm Gay. Harvest House Publishers, 2015. Kindle edition. 58.

[12] Allberry, Sam. Is God anti-gay? (Questions Christians Ask). The Good Book Company, 2013. Kindle edition. 9.

[13] Allberry, Sam. Is God anti-gay? (Questions Christians Ask). The Good Book Company, 2013. Kindle edition. 5.

[14] Perry, Jackie Hill. Gay Girl, Good God: The Story of Who I Was, and Who God Has Always Been. B&H Publishing Group, 2018. Kindle edition. 9.

[15] Yuan, Christopher; Yuan, Angela. Out of a Far Country. The Crown Publishing Group. Kindle Edition. 187.

[16] Yuan, Christopher; Yuan, Angela. Out of a Far Country. The Crown Publishing Group. Kindle Edition. 187.

[17] Butterfield, Rosaria. The Secret Thoughts of an Unlikely Convert: An English Professor's Journey into Christian Faith. Crown & Covenant Publications. Kindle Edition. 22.

[18] Allberry, Sam. Is God anti-gay? (Questions Christians Ask). The Good Book Company, 2013. Kindle edition. 34.

[19] Allberry, Sam. Is God anti-gay? (Questions Christians Ask). The Good Book Company, 2013. Kindle edition. 773.

[20] This proposition ended up costing both sides of the aisle just under a 100 million.

[21] Perry, Jackie Hill. Gay Girl, Good God: The Story of Who I Was, and Who God Has Always Been. B&H Publishing Group, 2018. Kindle edition. 62.

[22] Freedom In Christ Ministries www.ficm.org

[23] Gary J. Gates, Williams Distinguished Scholar. The Williams Institute, UCLA School of Law, April 2011.

[24] Barna, George. New Insights into the Generation of Growing Influence: Millennials in America. A Research Report by George Barna, Cultural Research Center at Arizona Christian University, October 2021.

[25] https://www.theblaze.com/news/san-francisco-gay-mens-chorus-pulls-video-threats?utm_source=dlvr.it&utm_medium=twitter

[26] Dallas, Joe. When Homosexuality Hits Home: What to Do When a Loved One Says, I'm Gay. Harvest House Publishers, 2015. Kindle edition. 23.

[27] https://www.desiringgod.org/embrace-the-life-god-has-given-you

[28] DesertStream.org